MANY FACES,
ONE CHURCH

General Editor: ROBERT A. LUDWIG

Sheed & Ward's **Catholic Studies Series** presents reader-friendly texts
to college classrooms and the broader community of faith and learning.
Authored by scholars committed to both solid academic content and the
lived experience of faith today, the books in the series are interdiscipli-
nary and represent the Catholic heritage in all its richness. Consistent
with Sheed & Ward's distinguished history, these books promise quality,
character, and an approach to the Catholic experience that is in tune
with the signs of the times.

MANY FACES, ONE CHURCH

Cultural Diversity and the American Catholic Experience

Edited by
PETER C. PHAN
and
DIANA HAYES

A SHEED & WARD BOOK
Lanham • Boulder • New York • Toronto • Oxford

A SHEED & WARD BOOK

ROWMAN & LITTLEFIELD PUBLISHERS, INC.

Published in the United States of America
by Rowman & Littlefield Publishers, Inc.

A wholly owned subsidary of The Rowman & Littlefield Publishing Group, Inc.
4501 Forbes Boulevard, Suite 200, Lanham, Maryland 20706
www.rowmanlittlefield.com

PO Box 317
Oxford OX2 9RU, UK

Elms College
291 Springfield Street, Chicopee, Massachusetts 01013

Copyright © 2005 by Rowman & Littlefield Publishers, Inc.

British Library Cataloguing in Publication Information Available

Library of Congress Cataloging-in-Publication Data
Many faces, one church : cultural diversity and the American Catholic
experience / edited by Peter C. Phan and Diana Hayes.
    p. cm.
"A Sheed & Ward book."
Includes bibliographical references and index.
ISBN 0-7425-3213-5 (alk. paper)—ISBN 0-7425-3214-3 (pbk. : alk.
paper)
    1. Catholic Church—United States. 2. Christianity and culture—United
States. I. Phan, Peter C., 1943– II. Hayes, Diana L.
    BX1406.3.M365 2005
    282'.73—dc22

                                                2004007059

Printed in the United States of America

♾ ™ The paper used in this publication meets the minimum requirements of
American National Standard for Information Sciences—Permanence of Paper for
Printed Library Materials, ANSI/NISO Z39.48-1992.

In grateful memory of
Joachim William Froehlich (1944–2003),
Eighth President of Elms College (2001–2003)

CONTENTS

FOREWORD

Something exciting is happening on the landscape of U.S. theology. With increasing frequency schools and departments of theology in the United States are welcoming to their faculty a new generation of theologians who come from ethnically and culturally diverse communities. These theologians include—but are not limited to—Asians, Blacks, Hispanics (Latino/as), and people from the Caribbean. Some of them were born and educated in the United States. Most, however, were born outside the United States and came to this country only later, bringing with them a different experience of church and a vast range of theological education at foreign universities.

Regardless of where they were born or educated, several of these theologians now occupy prestigious faculty and administrative positions in U.S. colleges, seminaries, and universities. The names of Gerald Boodoo, Diana Hayes, Roberto Goizueta, Peter Phan, and Jeanette Rodriguez, just to mention a few whose chapters appear in this volume, have found their rightful place in academic catalogs alongside those of other well-known Anglo-American theologians.

The Catholic Theological Society of America, College Theology Society, and other learned societies continue to add to their ranks this new group of theologians. Some of them have risen to leadership positions in these societies and have played an important role in shaping new directions in theology. Of special significance is the founding of the Academy of Catholic Hispanic Theologians of the United States (ACHTUS) in 1988. This theological society and other professional associations of minority theologians are a promising sign that multicultural theologies and theologians are here to stay.

With this new generation of theologians on the landscape of U.S. theology, a wave of theological innovation is being inaugurated as they assume responsibilities in the education of future ministers—both ordained and non-ordained—in the U.S. Church. They have mentored a new generation of Anglo-American theologians—including Kevin Burke, S.J., a contributor to this volume, and myself—in new ways of doing theology. In their interaction with students and colleagues at every level of theological and pastoral education, and through their teaching and their by now numerous publications, this new breed of theologians has made a lasting impact on the church and theology.

During the summers of 2001, 2002, and 2003 Elms College was delighted to welcome to our campus pastoral agents, religious, and clergy to three-day "Learning Festivals" devoted to the theme of multicultural theology. In addition to attending formal lectures by our distinguished presenters, participants were entertained by musicians representing the diverse cultural and ethnic groups living in the Diocese of Springfield and enjoyed meals featuring the native cuisine of these groups. Priests ministering in multicultural parish settings presided at our liturgies and members of their parishes performed various liturgical functions.

On behalf of my colleagues in the Religious Studies Department at Elms College, I express our sincere gratitude to all who participated in our summer learning festivals. In a very special way, I thank our presenters whose chapters appear in this volume for helping those of us living in the relatively quiet and isolated corner of Western Massachusetts to name and celebrate the diversity that characterizes our local church and to embrace the new "others" living in our midst.

On a more personal note, I extend a very special word of appreciation and thanks to Dr. Peter C. Phan, the Ignacio Ellacuría, S.J. Professor of Catholic Social Thought at Georgetown University, for his kindness and guidance since my student days at The Catholic University of America. It was with Peter's encouragement and direction that the summer learning festivals at Elms College were planned and executed. Peter's frequent presence at Elms College as lecturer and visiting professor continues to be a source of great blessings to the entire college community.

This book is dedicated to the memory of Dr. Joachim William Froehlich, the eighth president of the College of Our Lady of the Elms. We mourn his premature death and miss his all-too-short presidency at

Elms College. In less than twenty-six months he has left a permanent imprint on the college with his vision of education as preparation for leadership in faith communities. Because of this vision, he lent his enthusiastic support for the Elms Learning Festivals, even at substantial financial costs. We all owe Dr. Froehlich a heavy debt of gratitude and pray that his vision will continue to guide Elms College and the church for many years to come.

Mark Stelzer
Acting President
Elms College

INTRODUCTION: THE NEW FACES OF THE AMERICAN CATHOLIC CHURCH

Peter C. Phan

The American Catholic Church has been justly described as, in the words of church historian Jay P. Dolan, an "institutional immigrant." While the immigrant character of the U.S. Catholic Church appeared most pronounced after the 1820s with the arrival of large numbers of European immigrants, with time its face as a mosaic of different ethnic groups became blurred, especially after World War II, as American Catholics merged into the economic and political mainstream of America. This Americanization of U.S. Catholicism has been a long, gradual, and at times fiercely opposed process. The American Catholic Church, which was often portrayed as a foreign transplant, mainly from conservative European churches, ill-suited to the American ideals of religious freedom, separation of church and state, and religious pluralism, was, it is said, able, by dint of accommodation and struggle, to become truly American in the second half of the twentieth century.[1] By the mid-1960s, Catholics, who had been for the most part poor and uneducated blue-collar workers, were as well educated as other Americans, and as a group, would be indistinguishable from Americans as a whole. With the election of John F. Kennedy, the first Catholic president of the United States, the Americanization process of the American Catholic Church was completed: to be a faithful Catholic and a loyal American were now one and the same thing. In the words of church historian David O'Brien, "spurred by postwar educational and economic opportunities, millions of second- and third-generation Catholics had entered the middle class and moved to the suburbs."[2]

With this Americanization process, coupled with a drastically reduced European immigration in the 1920s (after the 1924 Reed-Johnson

Act which limited the number of European immigrants to 153,714 per annum) and the ban on Asian immigration (the 1882 Chinese Exclusion Act, reaffirmed in 1924), the immigration era of the American Catholic Church is said to be over. Speaking of the American Catholic Church in the late 1960s, O'Brien writes about how its immigrant era has come to an end: "American Catholicism had been shaped by the three factors of the conservative, dogmatic, and authoritative ultramontane church, the fluid social structure and stable democracy of the United States, and its own experience as an immigrant people. *Now the immigrant era was over*"[3] (emphasis added).

OTHER GROUPS IN THE AMERICAN CATHOLIC CHURCH AND CONTINUING IMMIGRATION

This version of the history of American Catholicism, with its Americanization thesis, perhaps unobjectionable in its outline, needs to be challenged, on at least two grounds. First, it assumes that the American Catholic Church from its inception was exclusively White and European, and more precisely, Irish and German. The hierarchy was dominated by these two ethnic groups, and the much-vaunted upward mobility of the American Catholic population was disproportionately represented by them. Missing from this picture is the story of Catholics of other European extracts such as the Italians, the Poles, the Lithuanians, the Czechs, and the Slovaks, and Eastern-rite Catholics, who not rarely were marginalized both within and without the church.

More tragic, from the perspective of this book, is the near-complete erasure of the older presence of native Mexican Catholics and African American Catholics in the country. It is only recently that the history of these two groups of American Catholics has been told, their contributions highlighted, their witnesses recognized.[4] But even now, their histories have not yet made it to the central pages of standard textbooks on American Catholicism. If mentioned at all, their presence is reported as a recent (and perhaps problematic) addition, and not as something important already present at the birth of the American Catholic Church.[5] Missing too from the common narrative is an account of Asian American Catholics, especially the Chinese, the Japanese, and the Filipinos, of the nineteenth and early twentieth centuries.[6] Their absence from American church history is all the more poignant since Asians were until 1952 designated "aliens ineligible for citizenship." Last but not least, absent too are the faces of Native American Catholics with whom missionaries had been in contact already since 1529.[7]

Second, the standard account of the Americanization of American Catholicism prematurely presumes that with the end of European immigration, the immigrant phase of American Catholicism is over.[8] Contrary to the prediction of most demographers that the flow of immigrants into the United States would trickle down after the restrictive laws of the 1920s, the country now receives near-record numbers of legal immigrants each year, and the second generation—those born in the United States with one or both parents born abroad—is larger than ever before. This dramatic increase of immigration is due to the Hart-Celler Act of 1965 and recent amendments to it, especially the Immigration Reform and Control Act of 1986 and the Immigration Act of 1990. Between 1920 and 1965 legal immigration to the United States averaged about 206,000 people per year, most of them from northern and western Europe. On the contrary, between the mid-1960s to the mid-1990s, the number of immigrants averaged over 500,000 per year, not counting undocumented immigrants.[9]

NON-EUROPEAN IMMIGRANTS IN THE UNITED STATES AND INTERCULTURAL THEOLOGY

What is of great significance in this unexpected phenomenon is that these new immigrants hail from parts of the world other than Europe and therefore bring with them challenges as well as resources vastly different from those of the still dominant White, Anglo-Saxon Americans, whether Catholic or Protestant.[10] Recently much publicity has been made of the findings of the 2000 census regarding the dramatic growth of the minority groups and their impact on the American society.

With regard to the influx of Hispanics into the United States, already in 1989, Allan Figueroa Deck referred to it as the "Second Wave."[11] According to the 2000 census, the Hispanic population increased by more than 50 percent since 1990, of which Mexicans constitute 58.5 percent; Puerto Ricans, 9.6 percent; Cubans, 3.5 percent; Central Americans, 4.8 percent; South Americans, 3.8 percent; Dominicans, 2.2 percent; Spaniards, 0.3 percent; and all other Hispanics, 17.3 percent.[12] Native Mexicans aside, Hispanic immigrants came mainly from Mexico, Cuba, and Central America (in particular El Salvador, Guatemala, and Nicaragua).

Asians too have experienced an enormous increase in the past decades. Prior to 1965, immigration from Asia, especially from the so-called Asian Pacific Triangle, had been prohibited on the basis of prejudices about the racial and ethnic inferiority and cultural unassimilability of Asians.[13] But things have changed drastically since then. During the last decade the Asian American population grew nearly 50 percent to reach a little more than 10 million in 2000. The five largest groups as reported by the 2000 census are: Chinese (2.4 million), Filipino (1.8 million), Indian (1.6 million), Vietnamese (1.1 million), and Korean (1.0 million). In addition to Hispanics and Asians, mention should be made of a significant number of immigrants from the Caribbeans and the Pacific Islands.

The changes in the origin, size, and composition of these newer immigrants have contributed to what has been called the "browning of America." As the authors of a recent study on these new immigrants put it, "These so-called new immigrants—those arriving in the post-1965 period—are phenotypically and culturally distinct from the old immigrants, who more closely resembled Anglo-Americans in terms of their physical characteristics and cultural patterns. . . . Moreover, research shows that the new immigrants are less inclined than the old immigrants to blend fully into American society. Most prefer, instead, to preserve and maintain their own cultural heritages and identities."[14] This shift is evidenced in the fact that instead of speaking of "assimilation," research on recent immigrants now refers to their "adaptation" to and "incorporation" into the American society which no longer possesses a single core culture but much more diverse cultural matrixes.[15]

It goes without saying that this recent immigration has had and will continue to have a profound and extensive impact on all sectors of the American society, not only in terms of what the United States as the receiving country has to do for these migrants, whether short-term, cyclical, or permanent,[16] but also in terms of the multiple benefits they indisputably bring to the American society. For good or for ill, the shape of the U.S. political, social, economic, cultural, and religious landscape has changed as the result of the massive presence of these non-European immigrants.

With regard to the religious arena in particular, it is well known that a great majority of Hispanics are Roman Catholic, though the Protestant, especially Pentecostal, presence is growing. Among Asian Americans, Roman Catholicism, though a tiny minority in Asia (except in the Philippines), has a significant membership. There is little doubt that the

American Churches, the Roman Catholic Church in particular, have been significantly affected in different ways by these new arrivals.

In terms of theology as an academic discipline, at least as it is practiced in the United States, the presence of non-European immigrants should have, and has begun to have, a significant impact on how theology is done, since theology, as is widely acknowledged today, must be contextual, and in this case, intercultural.[17]

The issue here is not simply the unfamiliar sources and resources, which are very different from those hitherto used by Western theologians, and from which intercultural theology will have to draw its materials, but more fundamentally, the very existential condition of the immigrant itself. In other words, the theologically important question concerns first and foremost the very nature of being an immigrant and refugee. This existential ontology of the immigrant entails a distinct epistemology and hermeneutics, a particular way of perceiving and interpreting reality, that is, oneself, others (in particular, the dominant others and fellow groups of immigrants), the cosmos, and ultimately, God.

THE NEW FACES IN AMERICAN CATHOLICISM AND INTERCULTURAL THEOLOGY

In the United States, given the many, culturally diverse ethnic groups that increasingly make up its population, theology must be done from their diverse social contexts and cultures. That is to say, a North American intercultural theology is not only a theology shaped by the encounter between *two* cultures, that is, the dominant (Anglo/European/White) culture and one other minority culture (e.g., Latino), but by the much more complex and challenging encounter of *several* cultures at the same time (e.g., Anglo and Latino and Black and Asian and Native American, and so on).[18] To express this point with prepositions, the encounter is not *between* but *among* cultures. The complexity of this theology will appear all the more daunting when one calls to mind that there is not a monolithic culture called Anglo, Latino, Black, Asian, and Native American but rather that each culture contains within itself several significant varieties and is itself an ever-changing and dynamic reality. Throw into this ethnic and cultural mix the gender component, and the shape of this intercultural theology becomes even more unwieldy.

The multicultural dialogue that shapes a theology out of the experience of migration is fortunately not foreign to many groups of immigrants in the United States but is an intrinsic part of their collective history. As Virgilio Elizondo has argued, the reality of *mestizaje* (the mixing of the Spanish and the Amerindian) and *mulataje* (the mixing of the Spanish and the African) is the fundamental characteristic of many Hispanics and thus makes interculturality a necessary matrix for Hispanic theology and church life.[19] This is no less true of African Americans, that is, Americans of African descent whose ancestry dated back to the period of slavery in the United States, and whose cultural lineage is traced, through the history of the slave trade, back to Africa (in particular West Africa), as well as of Black Americans, including recent immigrants from Africa, Central and South America, and the Caribbean. Their cultural and religious identity has been shaped by a long and painful encounter with the White supremacist culture and religion.[20] Asian Americans, too, bear within their history the mixture of cultures, in particular the Japanese, Koreans, and Vietnamese, who have absorbed, often by force, the Chinese/Confucian culture. Of course, this in-between cultural standing of these new non-European immigrants is exacerbated as they try to make their home in the United States, since they have to contend not only with the dominant Anglo/European/White culture but also with the cultures of fellow immigrant groups. A theology forged within this multicultural and multiethnic context will then be truly intercultural.

The collection of chapters here presented, as already mentioned in the preface, is made up of some of the papers presented at the "Learning Festivals" sponsored by Elms College. The intention of these conferences was to explore the reality of the "New Faces" of the American Catholic Church and its implications for our way of being church, our worship, and our theology. Some of these faces are by no means new: Mexicans and Blacks have been here from the very beginning. Others are newcomers, such as the people of various countries of Asia and the Caribbean. However, old or new, their voices have just been raised and heard, and their desire to live their Christian faith and to participate fully in the American Catholic Church has been heeded.

The present collection of essays makes no pretensions to covering all the issues—even the most important ones—posed by these ethnic Catholics to the American Catholic Church and theology. They simply highlight some of opportunities and challenges lying ahead as the American Church tries to respond to the presence of new immigrants in its midst. Mark Stelzer draws attention to the increasing presence of non-Anglo theologians teaching in U.S. Catholic colleges and universities and their contributions to Catholic theology. He also shows how the new theological method espoused by these theologians may be helpful in brokering a peaceful merging of national parishes that are no longer viable because of the dwindling membership of former ethnic parishioners. Kevin Burke, of Irish descent, reflects on how cultural diversity, which has always been a hallmark of American Catholicism, is a blessing for theology.

The remaining chapters give a bird-eye's view of the riches as well as the challenges that the "new faces" are bringing to the American Catholic Church. Diana Hayes recalls the history of Black Catholics in the United States and highlights five challenges facing Black Catholics and the church. Roberto S. Goizueta reflects on the contributions of Hispanic or Latino/a Catholicism, especially its popular religious practices, to Christian faith. Jeanette Rodriguez examines one practice dear to the hearts of all Mexican Americans, namely, the devotion to our Lady of Guadalupe, and its manifestations in worship. Peter C. Phan introduces the recent Catholic immigrants from Asia and the Pacific Islands and the distinctive cultural and religious gifts they bring to both the United States and the American Catholic Church. Finally, Gerard Boodoo reflects on the different ways of doing theology appropriate to the "forced context" of the Caribbean and on the *vocation*/calling of the church in these islands. We deeply regret that circumstances did not allow Elms College's "Learning Festivals" to include a lecture on Native American Catholics as planned. To make up for this lack we can only refer to some important studies on Native American religious traditions and theology.[21]

A welcome sign of a new awareness of the cultural and ethnic diversity in the church is the Encuentro 2000, sponsored by the National Conference of Catholic Bishops and held in Los Angeles, July 6–9, 2000, as a celebration of the Jubilee Year 2000. Subsequent to this encuentro the United States Catholic Conference of Bishops issued a statement entitled *Welcoming the Stranger Among Us: Unity in Diversity* (November 2000), which echoes the call of Pope John Paul II's Apostolic Exhortation *Ecclesia in America* to conversion, communion, and solidarity in the church's relations with its new ethnic groups. In a sense, these celebrations of the ethnic and cultural diversity in the American Catholic Church are but a festive prolongation of the manifold diversity already prevalent in the earliest years of American Catholicism. In another sense, however, it is also just a beginning of a long but exciting journey in which the strangers to be welcomed today into the bosom of the American Catholic Church will be themselves the hosts welcoming with equal warmth and generosity new strangers into their midst so that hosts and guests are truly one.

NOTES

1. For helpful surveys of American Catholicism, see Chester Gillis, *Roman Catholicism in America* (New York: Columbia University Press, 1999); Charles Morris, *American Catholic: The Saints and Sinners Who Built America's Most Powerful Church* (New York: Vintage Books, 1997); David J. O'Brien, *Public Catholicism* (Maryknoll, N.Y.: Orbis Books, 1996); Jay P. Dolan, *The American Catholic Experience: A History from Colonial Times to the Present* (Garden City, N.Y.: Doubleday, 1985); Jay P. Dolan, *In Search of American Catholicism: A History of Religion and Culture in Tension* (New York: Oxford University Press, 2002). For a collection of documents dealing with the American immigrant Catholic Church, see Jeffrey M. Burns, Ellen Skerrett, and Joseph M. White, eds., *Keeping Faith: European and Asian Catholic Immigrants* (Maryknoll, N.Y.: Orbis Books, 2000).

2. O'Brien, *Public Catholicism*, 232.

3. O'Brien, *Public Catholicism*, 234.

4. For a history of Black American Catholics, see Cyprian Davis, *The History of Black Catholics in the United States* (New York: Crossroad, 1992) and Cyprian Davis, "African American Catholics," in *The Encyclopedia of American Catholic History*, ed. Michael Glazier and Thomas Shelley (Collegeville, Minn.: The Liturgical Press, 1997), 6–13. For the Hispanic presence in the United States, see Moisés Sandoval, *On the Move: A History of the Hispanic Church in the United States* (Maryknoll, N.Y.: Orbis Books, 1990) and Jaime Vidal, "Hispanics Catholics in America," in *The Encyclopedia of American Catholic History*, 635–42.

5. I am not suggesting that standard works of American Church history ignore the presence of Black and Hispanic Catholics in American Catholicism as a whole. Rather, it is suggested that the Americanization thesis does not take into account their presence from the beginning of the American Catholic Church and throughout the whole process of Americanization.

6. On Asian Catholic immigrants, see Burnes et al., *Keeping Faith*, 229–307.

7. For an informative essay on Native American Catholics, see Carl F. Starkloff, "Native Americans and the Catholic Church," in *The Encyclopedia of American Catholic History*, 1009–20.

8. Again, I am not saying that standard works do not take into account the recent waves of Catholic immigrants. Indeed, Jay Dolan discusses at length the impact of these newcomers, mainly Hispanic and Asian, for the American Church. See his *In Search of an American Catholicism*, 211–24; 238–48. David O'Brien, in the second edition of his *Public Catholicism* (1996), acknowledges the presence of African American, Native American, and Spanish-speaking Catholics (he does not mention Asian Catholics), about whom almost nothing

is said even in the second edition. However, O'Brien says: "Each group deserved closer attention when I last wrote; each will need to play a central role in the story yet to be told" (x). The point I am making here is that the Americanization thesis assumes that, with the end of European immigration, the immigration of Catholics into the United States has ceased, marked by the closing of Ellis Island in 1955, the preeminent symbol of immigration.

9. Under the 1986 Immigration Reform and Control Act any illegal resident who could demonstrate that he or she had lived in the United States before 1982 was eligible to apply for citizenship. Three million undocumented aliens took advantage of this opportunity. At the end of the amnesty program in October 1988, it was estimated that 2.7 million illegal residents remained in the country who would provide the social networks for the coming of more illegal immigrants. During the decade of 1990–2000, according to the Immigration and Naturalization Service (INS), another 2.4 million immigrants have entered the United States illegally. The INS estimates that as of October 1996 there were five million illegal aliens living in the United States.

10. Before 1925, 85 percent of all international migrants originated in Europe, but since 1960 there has been a dramatic increase in emigration from Africa, Asia, and Latin America.

11. Allan Figueroa Deck, *The Second Wave: Hispanic Ministry and the Evangelization of Cultures* (New York: Paulist Press, 1989).

12. These figures are taken from the U.S. Census Bureau, compiled by Betsy Guzmán in an essay entitled "The Hispanic Population" (May 2001). In the census, by "people of Hispanic origin" are meant those whose origin was Mexican, Puerto Rican, Cuban, Central or South American, or some other Hispanic origin. The terms "Hispanic" or "Latino" are also used interchangeably.

13. Anti-Asian immigration legislation culminated in the Tydings-McDuffe Act of 1934 which can be traced back as far as the 1882 Chinese Exclusion Act, the Gentlemen's Agreement of 1908, and the 1917 and 1924 Immigration Acts. For an exposition of the American anxiety about the "Yellow Peril," see David Palumbo-Liu, *Asian/American: Historical Crossings of a Racial Frontier* (Stanford: Stanford University Press, 1999), 31–42.

14. James H. Johnson Jr., Walter C. Farrell, and Chandra Guinn, "Immigration Reform and the Browning of America: Tensions, Conflicts, and Community Instability in Metropolitan Los Angeles," in *The Handbook of International Migration*, ed. Charles Hirschman, Philip Kasinitz, and Josh DeWind (New York: Russell Sage Foundation, 1999), 391.

15. See Richars Alba and Victor Nee, "Rethinking Assimilation Theory for a New Era of Immigration," in *The Handbook of International Migration*, 137–160; Herbert J. Gans, "Toward a Reconciliation of 'Assimilation' and 'Pluralism': The Interplay of Acculturation and Ethnic Retention," in *The Handbook of International Migration*, 161–71; Rubén G. Rumbaut, "Assimilation and Its Discontents: Ironies and Paradoxes," in *The Handbook of International Migration*, 172–95; and

Min Zhou, "Segmented Assimilation: Issues, Controversies, and Recent Research on the New Second Generation," in *The Handbook of International Migration*, 196–211.

16. A study published by the Rand Corporation in November 1985 entitled *Current and Future Effects of Mexican Immigration in California* suggests that there are three types of Mexican immigrants: short-term (usually tied with agricultural, seasonal jobs), cyclical (with regular returns to the same employers), and permanent (usually with families settled in the United States). See Deck, *The Second Wave*, 12–15.

17. On the multicultural and intercultural character of contemporary theology, see the following works: Robert Schreiter, *Constructing Local Theologies* (Maryknoll, N.Y.: Orbis Books, 1985); Schreiter, *The New Catholicity: Theology Between the Global and the Local* (Maryknoll, N.Y.: Orbis Books, 1997); and Stephen Bevans, *Models of Contextual Theology* (Maryknoll, N.Y.: Orbis Books, 1992. It is well known that Hispanic/Latino theology, with its own professional association and journal, has emerged as a voice to be reckoned with. To a lesser extent, Asian American theology has begun to contribute to the theological enterprise in the United States.

18. This point has been made by María Pilar Aquino in "Theological Method in U.S. Latino/a Theology: Toward an Intercultural Theology for the Third Millennium," in *From the Heart of Our People: Latino/a Explorations in Catholic Systematic Theology*, ed. Orlando Espín and Miguel H. Díaz (Maryknoll, N.Y.: Orbis Books, 1999), 24–25: "U.S. Latino/a theology may not renounce its intercultural cradle. This is a theology born within a reality where a number of religious traditions and several theological formulations converge. European, Latin American, European-American, Afro-Latin and African American, Native American, and feminist traditions and elaborations have been welcome and critically embraced."

19. See Virgilio Elizondo, *The Galilean Journey: The Mexican-American Promise* (Maryknoll, N.Y.: Orbis Books, 1983); *The Future is Mestizo: Life Where Cultures Meet* (Oak Park, Ill.: Meyer-Stone Books, 1988); original French edition, *L'Avenir est au métissage* (Paris: Nouvelles Éditions Mame, 1987). See also his earlier two-volume work, *Mestizaje: The Dialectic of Cultural Birth and the Gospel* (San Antonio, Tex.: Mexican American Cultural Center, 1978), which is the English translation of his doctoral dissertation presented at the Institut Catholique, Paris, *Métissage, Violence culturelle, Annonce de l'Évangile: La Dimension interculturelle de l'Évangelisation*. It is interesting to note that the mixed race (*mestizaje*)—the *raza cósmica*—had been proposed by José Vasconcelos as a new era of humanity occurring in the Aesthetic Age. Such a *raza cósmica*, according to Vasconcelos, is already present in the peoples of Latin America insofar as they incorporate in themselves the Indian, European, and African "races." See his *The Cosmic Race/La raza cósmica*, trans. with introduction D. T. Jean (Baltimore and London: Johns Hopkins University Press, 1979).

20. See in particular Gayraud S. Wilmore, *Black Religion and Black Radicalism: An Interpretation of the Religious History of African Americans,* third edition (Maryknoll, N.Y.: Orbis Books, 1998); *Black Theology: A Documentary History, Volume I, 1966–79,* ed. James H. Cones and Gayraud S. Wilmore (Maryknoll, N.Y.: Orbis Books, 1993); and *Black Theology: A Documentary History, Volume 2, 1980–1992,* ed. James H. Cones and Gayraud S. Wilmore (Maryknoll, N.Y.: Orbis Books, 1993).

21. See *Native American Religious Identity: Forgotten Gods,* ed. Jace Weaver (Maryknoll, N.Y.: Orbis Books, 1998); Clara Sue Kidwell, Homer Noley, and George E. "Tink" Tinker, eds., *A Native American Theology* (Maryknoll, N.Y.: Orbis Books, 2001); James Treat, ed., *Native and Christian: Indigenous Voices on Religious Identity in the United States and Canada* (New York and London: Routledge, 1996); Marie Therese Archambault, Mark G. Thiel, and Christopher Vecsey, eds., *The Crossing of the Two Roads: Being Catholic and Native in the United States* (Maryknoll, N.Y.: Orbis Books, 2003).

1

A NEW ECCLESIAL REALITY
AND A NEW WAY OF DOING
THEOLOGY: HERALDING
A NEW PENTECOST

Mark Stelzer

It is by now a well-known sociological fact that both the United States and the American Catholic Church are undergoing a significant demographic shift. The so-called minority groups are growing rapidly and their presence is posing all kinds of challenges as well as opening up new opportunities for both society and church. In the American Catholic Church in particular, while the shrinking number of European Catholics has forced the closing, merging, or yoking of many "national parishes," the arrival of new immigrants from Asia, Africa, and Latin America has changed the face of the church. Of course, these newcomers have brought with them their distinctive cultural and religious gifts, not least among which is a new way of doing theology. This chapter studies one of the current challenges posed by the new demographic shift, namely, the merging of national parishes, and explores how the new way of doing theology can be useful in negotiating the painful and tension-filled process of closing down and merging of parishes.

This chapter proceeds in three steps. First, we discuss the changing context of theological and pastoral education today and show how it has challenged theologians and pastoral agents to embrace those living at the borders of church and society. Next, we review the history of the national parish system in the United States and indicate some of the factors that have led to the merging, yoking, or even suppression of parishes and as a result have made people crossing parish borders. Finally, we show how the theological method developed by the two Brazilian brothers Leonardo and Clodovis Boff can be used to respond effectively to the challenges of working collaboratively in parishes that were autonomous previously. Throughout the chapter, the impending merger of

Holy Name of Jesus Parish and Assumption Parish, both adjacent to Elms College, will serve as a case study.

THE CHANGING CONTEXT AND
THE CALL TO CROSS BORDERS

Vatican II: The Watershed Event

In the forty years since the Second Vatican Council (1962–1965), theological and pastoral education in the church has undergone a drastic change as seminaries, once a bastion of orthodoxy and a reliable training ground for doctrinally conservative clergy, have been awakened by the conciliar documents and a new generation of theologians from their "dogmatic slumber" that often allowed theology—and the God of whom theology speaks—to become arid, unintelligible, and remote.

Reflecting on his own theological journey, Spanish Jesuit theologian Jon Sobrino (b. 1938), who teaches in El Salvador, speaks of a "sleep of inhumanity" from which the postconciliar Church is gradually awakening.[1] The sleep of inhumanity to which Sobrino refers was induced by a theological and spiritual individualism that failed to imagine a church beyond the sacred spaces of its sanctuary, religious houses, or educational institutions. Only when the church's attempts at self-definition at Vatican II began to take into account the world beyond these time-honored places did the theological, religious, and ethical exigencies of a multicultural church become more apparent. In its Pastoral Constitution on the Church in the Modern World (*Gaudium et Spes*), the council declares: "Faithful to her own tradition and at the same time conscious of her universal mission, she [the church] can enter into communion with various cultural modes, to her own enrichment and to theirs too."[2]

In the late 1960s, French Dominican Yves Congar (1904–1995), one of the most prolific and influential theologians of the last century, said: "It is not unreasonable to suppose that one day our pagan continent might be re-evangelized by people of color, the pagans of yesterday, the Christians of today and tomorrow."[3] What Congar predicted for Europe has become a reality on our own continent. In the United States, Asian, Black, Latino/a theologians and those from other cultural and ethnic groups have challenged those of us living comfortably at the center to adopt a new vision of humanity, the world, and the church. In heralding a new Pentecost, this new generation of theologians rightly insists that this vision must be one that embraces—and is transformed by—the borders.

Jesus Crossing Borders

Mexican American theologian Virgilio Elizondo suggests that since its inception, Christianity has been a religion committed to crossing seemingly impenetrable borders for the sake of unity.[4] In the Incarnation, the Word of God crossed the border between the divine and human, between the eternal and the temporal. In the words of Paul, "Christ, though in the image of God, did not deem equality with God something to be grasped at. Rather he emptied himself and took the form of a slave, being born in our likeness" (Phil 2:6–7). In this famous hymn, Paul emphasizes that the self-emptying, or *kenosis*, that occurs in the Incarnation affirms that God belongs to the world of God's creatures.[5] Above all, Paul stresses that divinity manifests itself in humility and in service.

In his public ministry, Jesus constantly crossed established borders and embraced those who lived on the other side. From a simple conversation with the woman at the well (Jn 4:5–26) to table fellowship shared with a tax collector (Mk 2:15–17), Jesus crossed borders and in the process confronted the social and religious biases of his time. All this he did with conviction that a truly universal human family not divided on ethnic, religious, or linguistic lines is truly possible and desirable.[6]

Nowhere in the New Testament is border crossing more obvious than in the Pentecost event (Acts 2:1–13). As recorded by Luke, the event of Pentecost challenged the religious and social prejudices and practices of the time. Women and men, Jews and Greeks, believers and nonbelievers alike, heard the preaching of the apostles and understood them in their own tongues. Enlightened by the Spirit, the disciples learned that to follow Jesus, one must take risks and cross borders. Moving from behind the safety and security of locked doors where they lived in fear, the disciples, empowered by the Holy Spirit, went forth from Jerusalem, beyond the borders of their world, to embrace the unknown others.

Border Crossing Today: A Reverse Movement

Although the history of Christianity points to painful periods of division and even bloodshed, Elizondo stresses that the original Christian spirit of reaching out to rather than fearing others is a great contribution that

Christianity continues to offer the human family at the beginning of the third Christian millennium. In the meantime, however, a significant shift has occurred. Whereas since the first Pentecost Christian missionaries have traveled to unknown parts of the world to evangelize them, today a reverse movement is taking place. With increasing frequency local churches are challenged to welcome the strangers who now enter into their borders, mindful of the Gospel teaching that to welcome the stranger is to welcome Christ (Mt 25:35).

Nowhere is this demographic shift more obvious than in U.S. parishes that are struggling to welcome persons of diverse cultural, ethnic, and linguistic backgrounds who are arriving in great numbers at their borders. Although theologians and pastoral agents justifiably focus their considerable attention on the challenges posed by the presence of newer immigrants such as Asian and Hispanic Catholics, we must not forget a concurrent challenge facing the church as older immigrant groups such as French Canadian Catholics and Polish Catholics, who once found comfort and security in the so-called national parishes and territorial parishes defined by geographic boundaries, now find themselves at each other's borders.

Usually under the pressure caused by a shortage of clergy or declining church membership and financial support, national and territorial parishes most often arrive at each other's borders. There is a diocesan mandate for these parishes to merge into one consolidated parish or—at a minimum—to operate as yoked parishes that will share the time and resources of one priest or pastoral team.

Since other chapters in this volume will address the specific challenges posed to U.S. parishes by new immigrant groups such as the Asians, the Hispanics, the Pacific Islanders who arrive daily at their borders, this chapter will focus on some of the dynamics involved as members of national parishes and of territorial parishes arrive at each other's borders. We begin by looking briefly at the history and dynamics of the national parish system.

THE NATIONAL PARISH: THEN AND NOW

Common Trends and Practices

As Kevin Burke points out, even the most casual reading of history makes it apparent that for the U.S. Church cultural diversity is nothing new. Not only is cultural diversity not new, it has left its indelible mark on the U.S. Catholic experience.[7]

As we know well from the history of the Diocese of Springfield, U.S. bishops responded to the presence of diverse cultures by creating an impressive system of national parishes. In this system, one cultural group was served by a parish that celebrated the Eucharist and other sacraments in their native language. These parishes also preserved their members' cultural heritage through festivals, devotions, Catholic schools, and other programs of religious instruction. Because people tended to live in small urban neighborhoods already defined along ethnic, cultural, and linguistic lines, these parishes often arose naturally, without explicit pastoral planning. However, as members of the second or third generations of immigrants moved out of their closely knit urban neighborhoods and out of their ethnic parishes, national parishes were intentionally created as pastoral means to allow members of these younger generations to travel beyond their local territorial parishes to participate in the life of so-called French, Italian, Polish, or German parishes.

Today, the edifices of national parishes stand as poignant reminders of the marvelous diversity that has always been a dominant characteristic of the U.S. Catholic Church. The buildings of these parishes, beside the churches, often sprawled over an entire city block and served as grammar schools, high schools, social centers, convents, and rectories. Collectively, these structures remind us of the sacrifice and dedication of the laity, religious, and clergy who instinctively recognized that the work of nurturing the Body of Christ entailed more than the celebration of the sacraments and must embrace the social, educational, and economic needs of a growing immigrant population. As a case in point, we need look no further than the Elms campus and its two neighboring parishes.

Holy Name Parish and Assumption Parish: A Case Study

Adjacent to Elms College stand two parish churches: Holy Name and Assumption. Holy Name of Jesus Parish, where I presently serve as pastor, was founded in 1838 to serve the needs of Irish immigrants. When the young parish outgrew a small wooden church on a remote side street, an impressive cathedral-like church was built in 1859 on one of Chicopee's most prestigious streets. Within just a few years, a rectory, a school, a convent, and a residence for teaching brothers became part of a sprawling parish campus.

Priests assigned to Holy Name of Jesus Parish soon began to serve the spiritual needs of French Canadians who were arriving in Chicopee in great numbers in the last decades of the nineteenth century. So great was the influx of French Canadians that Assumption of the Blessed Virgin Parish was established in 1885 with the specific charge of ministering to the spiritual needs of this growing community. Within a matter of only a few years, Assumption Parish built a stately Romanesque church just one block south of Holy Name Church, established a parish school, and acquired the homes of two very prominent private citizens for use as a convent and the rectory. Less than 1,000 yards from each other, there soon stood two churches, two rectories, two schools, two convents, and a residence to house the Irish Christian Brothers who were teaching grammar school boys at Holy Name Parish.

To read the histories of Holy Name Parish and Assumption Parish is to delight in stories of vibrant communities whose life centered around the sacraments, the parish school, and parish organizations. Groups like the Legion of Mary, Sacred Heart League, Children of Mary, and Holy Name Society were an integral part of life in both parishes. Parish athletic leagues, scouting troops, and even musical bands instilled in young people a sense of pride and often encouraged inter-parish rivalry.

Well into the 1960s, Holy Name Parish and Assumption Parish were thriving, autonomous communities. Holy Name Parish rejoiced in the election of John F. Kennedy who epitomized the hopes and dreams of all American-born Irish. The church and convent underwent extensive and costly renovation. Many priests assigned to Holy Name held doctoral degrees and taught on a full- or part-time basis at the Elms College.

At Assumption Parish, Masses and other sacraments continued to be celebrated regularly in French. Priests assigned to Assumption Parish remained part of the "French League," a group of diocesan priests of French Canadian descent traditionally assigned only to French national parishes. Given the prestige of the parish, appointment to the pastorate of Assumption Parish was reserved for priests who had distinguished themselves in previous pastorates.

The changes in church and society that occurred in the last decades of the twentieth century had a great impact on Holy Name Parish and Assumption Parish. The growing expenses of operating a parish high school resulted in the merger of Holy Name High School with Sacred Heart High School in nearby Springfield in 1977. Because Sacred Heart High School had the larger facility, it was decided that the newly merged school would operate on the Springfield campus. Although Holy Name

Grammar School remained open, the loss of the parish high school dealt a severe blow to the morale of parishioners and graduates alike.

At Assumption Parish, changing demographics in the City of Chicopee resulted in a sharp decline in the number of new parishioners of French Canadian descent. At the same time, a new generation of younger parishioners had little, if any, knowledge of French. For these reasons the number of Masses celebrated in French gradually decreased. With the need for religious and secular instruction in French nearly eliminated, the viability and expenses of operating a parish grammar school where some classes used to be taught in French were questioned. Following considerable discernment and some very lean years, Assumption School closed in 1991. Soon afterwards, the Daughters of the Holy Spirit, who had conducted the parish school from its earliest days, decided to return to their motherhouse in Connecticut. The departure of the Sisters and the stark reality of a vacated school and convent were a clear and painful signal that Assumption Parish was facing a time of transition like its neighbor Holy Name Parish.

At the time of my appointment as pastor of Holy Name Parish in December 2002, diocesan officials urged parishioners of Holy Name Parish and Assumption Parish to begin a process of collaboration in anticipation of the day when they will be served only by one priest. After his seventy-fifth birthday, Father Gerry Lafleur, the young-hearted pastor of Assumption Parish, planned to remain in active ministry until his eightieth birthday. In the meantime, he enthusiastically welcomed the opportunity to prepare his parishioners for his retirement and for the day when Holy Name Parish and Assumption Parish would operate as merged or yoked parishes. Given the proximity of the two parishes to the Elms College, diocesan officials also suggested that the two parishes work closely with college administrators, religious studies faculty, and campus ministers to provide educational opportunities and social gatherings designed to prepare parishioners and members of the college community to work as a unified faith community in Chicopee's Historic District.

Through programs facilitated by the Institute for Theology and Pastoral Studies at Elms College, parish leaders at Holy Name and Assumption have the opportunity to meet regularly to explore creative models for parish mergers. As regular participants in a summer learning festival at Elms College focused on a particular theological theme from a multicultural perspective, parishioners have also been exposed to the changing agenda and models of theology in an increasingly diverse Church.

In the next section, I discuss a model of theological reflection developed by two Brazilian brothers, Leonardo and Clodovis Boff, that may be used to assist parishes like Holy Name and Assumption in working collaboratively together. Consisting of socio-analytic, hermeneutical, and practical mediations, this method can be adapted to virtually any context in which theologians and pastoral agents have to minister in an increasingly diverse Church.

THREE THEOLOGICAL MEDIATIONS: A THEOLOGICAL METHOD

In the 1980s, Leonardo and Clodovis Boff wrote a very short, but significant, book entitled *Introducing Liberation Theology*.[8] In it the authors offer a helpful overview of the major themes and challenges of liberation theology. Particularly useful for our purposes is their discussion of theological method. Although developed as a specific response to the struggles of the church in Latin America, the theological method proffered by the Boff brothers can be successfully translated and applied to other cultural and religious settings. In this section, we reflect on how this method works and suggest ways in which this method can be applied as parish leaders and parishioners at Holy Name Parish and Assumption Parish attempt to transcend historical and cultural differences in an effort to build a unified faith community.

Preliminary Stage: Living Commitment

According to the Boffs, a living commitment of faith must precede the doing of theology. For this reason, the preliminary stage of their method is called "pre-theological" insofar as it stresses that before doing theology a theologian must first experience a conversion of life that comes from some form of contact with those for whom theology is being written. Although different forms or levels of contact can be taken up, ranging from sporadic visits or meetings with groups to permanent residency and work alongside a particular group, one point is clear: theology must begin with some living engagement with a Christian community.

In most dioceses, the process leading to the yoking or merging of parishes is precipitated by the transfer or death of a resident pastor. Although rumors of an impending merger may have circulated for months or years, the fact remains that most parish mergers are effected during a period of emotional unrest in the parish. Often, parishioners are still actively grieving the loss of their pastor when the bureaucratic and canonical process of merger or even suppression of their parish begins. A "new" priest is appointed to serve as pastor of the merged parishes—most often the pastor of a neighboring parish. Unavoidably, he is regarded with suspicion by still-grieving parishioners who fear that what is about to take place is more a "takeover" than a merger.

Clearly, what is lacking in such instances is a period of "living engagement" during which a priest/pastoral team come to know the people to whom they will minister and with whom they will be invited to articulate a theological and pastoral vision for the newly merged parish. This living engagement need not be excessively formal or programmed. In the case of Holy Name Parish and Assumption Parish, diocesan foresight in pastoral planning has afforded me the opportunity to come to know the parishioners of Assumption and their concerns prior to any official diocesan intervention. By attending social functions at the other's parish and through mealtime conversation on a regular basis, Father Gerry Lafleur, pastor of Assumption, and I are gradually learning the hopes and fears of our parishioners during this time of impending transition.

Stage One: Socio-Analytic Mediation

Although the primary object of theology is God, theologians must first begin by informing themselves about the actual conditions in which people live. However, before making assumptions about what the concrete circumstances of individuals or communities mean in God's eyes, theologians must first ask more basic questions about how a particular situation came to be. For this reason, an important part of socio-analytic mediation is a study of the history and the historical process of which individuals and communities are a part.

As noted above, Holy Name Parish and Assumption Parish enjoy very prestigious histories. As the mother church of the Diocese of Springfield, the original boundaries of Holy Name Parish included all four counties of Western Massachusetts. Assumption Parish, one of the finest in the French League, was built high on a hill and served as an icon of the success of French Canadian Catholics in Chicopee. Both parishes are justifiably proud of their pasts. Nonetheless, a study of the history of these two parishes and of the historical process of which they remain a part reveals a certain degree of mutual prejudice and suspicion. Although such tendencies are quite subtle, it is not uncommon even today to hear parishioners refer to Holy Name as the "Irish parish" or to Assumption as the "French parish." Despite the fact that the churches are located on the same city block, many parishioners of Holy Name have never been inside Assumption Church and vice-versa. In an effort to overcome such prejudice and suspicion a conscious effort is being made through a series of bulletin articles and adult education sessions to trace the history of Catholicism in Chicopee. In this process, parishioners of both parishes have been encouraged to learn that in their early years Holy Name and Assumption shared many resources in common, including an Irish-born, French-speaking priest assigned to Holy Name Parish who ministered to French-Canadian immigrants.

The relatively recent histories of the parishes also point to a period of considerable tension when changing demographics forced the closing of Assumption School which, like Holy Name School, had provided instruction from kindergarten through grade eight. Although many Assumption parishioners hoped to effect a consolidation of Assumption School and Holy Name School whereby Assumption would become an elementary school housing pre-kindergarten through grade four and Holy Name would become a middle school housing the remaining upper grades, the suggestion was not accepted by Holy Name parishioners who successfully insisted on maintaining a pre-kindergarten through grade eight school.

Stage Two: Hermeneutical Mediation

Once theologians have understood the concrete historical situation in which they have immersed themselves, they must ask: "What does the Word of God say about this situation?" Insofar as it is a question of seeing concrete reality in the light of faith and in the light of God's Word, discourse at this second stage is formally theological.

At this stage, Christian theologians turn to the Bible which they read "not as a book of strange stories, but as a book of life."[9] In this process emphasis is not placed so much on interpreting the text of the scriptures as "interpreting life according to the scriptures"[10] In their reading of the scriptures, Christian theologians seek to discover and activate the liberating message of the biblical texts as it applies to the concrete situation in which they find themselves.

It must be stressed that for Christian theologians, the Bible is not the only text in light of which concrete human reality is to be interpreted. Church teaching, in particular the decrees of ecumenical councils, must be critically studied in an effort to determine what light they might shed on contemporary circumstances. Additionally, the lives of countless saints, prophets, and holy women and men of all ages must be read as "texts" capable of helping theologians better understand the present situation they seek to interpret.

In the case of parishes like Holy Name and Assumption, the Eucharist and its invitation to communion are not only a "text" that parishioners and leaders must "read" as they venture into new models of collaboration; they are also the context within which changes are explained and carried out. Although representative committees of parishioners spend considerable time and energy outside the context of worship organizing and planning for the future, it is in the context of the liturgy of the Lord's Day with the entire assembly gathered that presiders and lay leaders enlighten and inform parishioners about the transitions taking place. Hopefully, they do so by appealing to the meaningful theological themes that have informed concrete decisions regarding activities of parish life. These usually include a new Mass schedule, the future use of parish buildings, and the amalgamation of the fiscal assets and/or liabilities both parishes bring to the merger.

Three theological themes have inspired parish leaders at Holy Name and Assumption in preparing parishioners to work collaboratively. They are Trinity, Incarnation, and grace. Deeply rooted in scripture and tradition, these themes find expression in liturgical texts and have implicitly informed pastoral praxis through the centuries.

TRINITY

Pointing to a mystery of communion and mutuality, the trinitarian doctrine of God provides, in the words of Catherine LaCugna, the "critical principle against which we can measure present institutional arrangements."[11] Because the nature of the church must manifest the nature of God, every effort in the merging or yoking of parishes must enflesh the inclusiveness, interdependence, and cooperation that characterize the inner life of the triune God.

INCARNATION

As already suggested, a prevalent metaphor for explaining the Incarnation in our times is "border crossing." More than a simple passing over a line of demarcation, the border crossing which theologians point to in the Incarnation is one that invites us to embrace the other. It is vitally important to note that in this process we embrace the other precisely as other and not as one who must be changed to look, think, act as we do. This is an incredibly helpful insight for those who labor under a common mindset that constantly looks for ways to make realities—in this case two parishes—converge and somehow look alike.[12]

GRACE

Finally, the theme of grace reminds us of the constant self-communication of God in the concrete events of daily living.[13] Because it is usually implicit and unthematic, God's self-communion frequently goes unnoticed or is ignored. For this reason, the challenge to pastoral agents is to help others notice, understand, and accept individual and communal experiences of God's self-communication. In this regard, it is important to note that not all of experiences of God are positive. Negative experiences, including fear of the unknown and the many losses that often accompany the consolidation of parish communities, are also moments in which God's grace comes to us as an invitation to embrace the unknown future in faith.

Stage Three: Practical Mediation

Having faithfully analyzed a given historical context in light of the Bible and the Tradition, the theologian is moved to action. Not content to remain in the realm of theory, theologians will work with pastoral agents to define strategies and tactics that will promote "the work of love, conversion, renewal of the Church, and transformation of society."[14] In the work of practical mediation, every effort is made to coordinate micro-actions of individuals and small communities with the macro-system of large structures and organizations.

For parish communities engaged in a process of merging, it is at this stage that concrete actions are taken to implement structural changes that will support the theological vision articulated at stages one and two. It is usually at this stage that canonical procedures designed to officially effect the merger are undertaken.

In summary, the theological method proposed by the Boff brothers starts from action and leads to action. Beginning with a living commitment and solidarity with those for whom they do theology, theologians pass through the reading of relevant Christian texts, and finally arrive at specific actions. "Back to action" is the characteristic call of proponents of this method. Throughout this section, we have shown how this method is being successfully applied as parish leaders and parishioners at Holy Name and Assumption build together their future in faith.[15]

CONCLUSION

Diversity presents a challenge to the entire church. In the United States that challenge is being felt as parishes founded according to ethnic and linguistic differences are now forced by changing demographics in the church and society to operate as merged or yoked parishes.

According to concrete possibilities of individual dioceses, an extensive period of pastoral preparation and theological reflection prior to the canonical implementation of a merger or the less formal process of yoking of parishes should be made available. This period provides parish leaders and parishioners a necessary opportunity to explore their past, understand their present, and plan for their future together.

This chapter has shown how the model of theological and pastoral reflection proposed by Leonardo and Clodovis Boff can be successfully translated and applied to U.S. parishes which find themselves with increasing frequency at each other's borders. In this context, we pointed to the important themes of Trinity, Incarnation, and grace and the light they shed on concrete historical reality and pastoral praxis. In the next chapter Kevin Burke invites us to reflect on cultural diversity as a gift to theology. With that gift comes a task. A task to celebrate the diversity that surrounds us and to embrace borders with respect and reverence. Other contributions to this volume insist that this gift and task present a considerable challenge to U.S. theologians and pastoral agents as they lead others to the realization that in God's house there is "plenty good room."

NOTES

1. See Jon Sobrino, "Awakening from the Sleep of Inhumanity," in *The Principle of Mercy: Taking the Crucified People from the Cross*, trans. Dimas Planas (Maryknoll, N.Y.: Orbis Books, 1994), 1–11.

2. *Gaudium et Spes*, no. 58.

3. Yves Congar, *Christians in the World* (New York: Herder and Herder, 1968), 200.

4. See Virgilio Elizondo, *Christianity and Culture* (San Antonio, Tex.: Mexican American Cultural Center, 1975), 29.

5. On this point, see Lucien Richard, *Christ the Self-Emptying of God* (New York: Paulist Press).

6. See Elizondo, *Christianity and Culture*, 31.

7. See his chapter "Thinking about the Church: The Gift of Cultural Diversity to Theology" in this book.

8. Leonard Boff and Clodovis Boff, *Introducing Liberation Theology*, trans. Paul Burns (Maryknoll, N.Y.: Orbis Books, 1987).

9. Boff and Boff, *Liberation Theology*, 34.

10. Boff and Boff, *Liberation Theology*, 34.

11. Catherine Mowry LaCugna, *God for Us: The Trinity & Christian Life* (San Francisco: HarperSanFrancisco, 1991), 402.

12. On this, see David Power, "Communion within Pluralism in the Local Church: Maintaining Unity in the Process of Inculturation," in *The Multicultural Church: A New Landscape in U.S. Theologies*, ed. William Cenkner (New York: Paulist Press, 1996), 79–101.

13. On the theme of God's pervasive grace as divine self-communication, see the thought of Karl Rahner in *A World of Grace*, ed. Leo O'Donovan (New York: Seabury Press, 1980) and Michael Skelley, *The Liturgy of the World: Karl Rahner's Theology of Worship* (Collegeville, Minn.: The Liturgical Press, 1991).

14. Boff and Boff, *Liberation Theology*, 39.

15. For a fuller exposition of this method, see Peter C. Phan, "A Common Journey, Different Paths, the Same Destination: Method in Liberation Theologies," in *Christianity with an Asian Face* (Maryknoll, N.Y.: Orbis Books, 2003), 26–46.

2

THINKING ABOUT THE CHURCH: THE GIFT OF CULTURAL DIVERSITY TO THEOLOGY

Kevin F. Burke

> Whoever talks about God in Jesus' sense will always take into account the way one's own preformulated certainties are wounded by the misfortune of others.
>
> Johann Baptist Metz[1]

The central focus of this book, cultural diversity in the American Catholic experience, touches a wide range of issues. As such, it can influence a variety of disciplines, including cultural anthropology, sociology, philosophy, political science, economics, U.S. history, and Roman Catholic Church history. In this chapter I look at the way it affects and enriches the discipline of theology. I begin with the assumption that cultural diversity denotes both an historical and a theological reality. In the words of the Second Vatican Council, it represents a *sign of the times*.[2] Because "culture" decisively affects the inner life of Christians and the Christian community, cultural diversity represents an important topic for anyone interested in thinking about the church. At an even deeper level, cultural diversity influences theology and thus represents a potential "gift" to theology itself. By pursuing this latter point, I aim to show how the encounter with cultural diversity leads theology to new insights into the Christian faith. In the process, I note several characteristics of a theology capable of receiving and actualizing this gift.[3] However, I do not write primarily for theologians. Rather, I write for everyone interested in "thinking about the church." For the way we do theology in turn influences the structure of the church and touches the lives of its members.

I divide this chapter into three sections. First, I examine cultural diversity as an historical reality and note how, in the light of historical consciousness, it can function as a sign of the times. In section two, drawing on the work of Johann Baptist Metz and the category of "dangerous memory," I probe the underside of our experience of cultural diversity and expose the seduction of a "superficial recognition" of this reality. Here I assess what it costs people of faith to actually engage cultural "others." In the final section I note how cultural diversity reshapes theology, and how a theology capable of apprehending and responding to cultural diversity enriches our thinking about the church.

CULTURAL DIVERSITY
AS SIGN OF THE TIMES

I begin with four observations regarding cultural diversity. *First, cultural diversity itself is not new.* As a global statement touching on human experience in general, or the more particular history of the Roman Catholic Church, or the even more particular experience of Catholics in America, this observation hardly raises eyebrows or requires justification. A moment's reflection on the Catholic experience in America bears out the point. From the earliest Spanish and French missionaries and settlers to the Catholic minorities living in the English colonies, the converts among native peoples and African slaves, and the enormous waves of Catholic immigrants in the nineteenth century, down to the present, when Catholic communities from nearly every culture on earth can be found in the United States, the Catholic Church in America has embodied a multicultural tapestry. In his book *The American Catholic Experience*, historian Jay Dolan notes:

> As a world religion, Roman Catholicism had set its roots into many nations and cultures. Catholics could be found in the many countries of Europe and throughout the Middle East. But, within each nation, Catholicism was culturally quite homogeneous, with the native culture clearly the dominant force in the church. In the United States it would be quite different. Immigration brought millions of people from diverse cultures and backgrounds to these shores, and this posed a mighty challenge to both nation and church. People of different nationalities were mixed together, and somehow they had to adjust to the American way of life while preserving their own unique her-

itages. Unity had to be achieved in the midst of diversity. For the Catholic Church, this would prove to be a delicate balancing act, but its continued existence in the United States meant accomplishing this feat.[4]

American Catholicism has always included the many faces of different cultures, but those many faces have not always prayed together, worked together, or lived together. Intermarriage was discouraged between partners from different ethnic and racial groups, despite the fact that they belonged to the same church. For example, far from being one community, immigrant Catholics tended to live as discrete communities, often pejoratively referred to as "Catholic ghettos." They gravitated toward their own neighborhoods, built their own parishes, schools, labor unions, and social organizations, and drew inspiration from their own priests, community leaders, and patron saints. These communities were defined by ethnicity and, in time, increasingly by social-economic class and geographic region. As immigration in the twentieth century brought Catholics from many parts of the world—Eastern Europe, the Middle East, South and East Asia, Oceania, Latin America and the Caribbean, Africa, and other parts of Europe—the complex diversity of the American Catholic experience reached new heights. As long as there have been Catholics in America, cultural diversity has been a crucial element in their story.

Second, cultural particularity places its stamp on all of our lives. I demonstrate this with a personal example as a U.S. citizen of European Catholic ancestry. My forebears came from Ireland. My mother's grandparents came in the aftermath of the great famine in the middle of the nineteenth century. The parents of my paternal grandmother came in the latter part of that same century. Micky Burke, my father's father, came here in 1901. Unlike most Irish immigrants, he did not settle down on the east coast. Instead, he took a train west to work on a sheep ranch in central Wyoming in the years just after Wyoming had become a state. Granddad Burke eventually acquired his own ranch near Casper, where my father was born just as the United States entered World War I. My sisters and brothers and I were born and grew up in Wyoming during and after the Second World War. I mention this particular example to draw attention to something common to all people: we cannot think of our lives only in terms of ourselves and our own private experiences. Each of us represents a trajectory launched through personal choices— our own and others'—engendered in the context of familial, religious, ethnic, and other historical realities.

Inevitably there exist unknown or uncharted spans within the trajectories we are living. To continue with the example of my own family, I was told that all my ancestors on both sides of the family were Irish, but without an explanation as to how several English names sprouted on our family tree. Moreover, I eventually became aware that whenever I spoke about my Irish roots, I instinctively told Granddad Burke's story: how he grew up on a farm in West Cork before coming to the United States; how, in the beginning, he worked in an unpeopled wilderness and often had no one to talk to for weeks at a stretch; how he eventually built his own ranch, married twice and raised the children of two families; how he died at the age of eighty-nine when I was in eighth grade, the year after my own father ran for Governor of Wyoming, and so on. But lately I have become interested in the pressure exerted by the untold stories. What about the other branches of the family? What about those English names? And what about the women? I mention my father's father, but what about his mother, who died when he was a boy? What about her ancestors? And what about my mother's people, who came from other parts of Ireland?

Several years ago, I stood on the pier at Cobh, near Cork City. Most of the ships that bore Irish immigrants to America left from there. Today a museum stands near the pier honoring the Irish Diaspora, focusing a good deal of attention on the famous "potato famine" of the mid-nineteenth century. The realization overwhelmed me there that I, too, have a share in that powerful drama of survival. Yet those stories, the journeys of those ancestors, are lost to memory. Who were these women and men? What did they feel when they got on those boats? Did they harbor any realistic hope or desire of ever seeing their native place again? What was their faith like? Surely it lives on in me, but how in particular? And how did they see themselves in this new land? Did they experience discrimination in the United States, as many of their fellow Irish did? What did that do to them? I raise these questions because this particular family story—no more or less dramatic than countless other stories—calls attention to something larger than itself, namely, the narrative moment in the discipline of theology. I also want to note that I (we) have forgotten, have lost, or have been robbed of some of my (our) most important stories. In this light, the exercise of *memory* will prove crucial, a point to which I will return in the second section of this chapter below.

This brings me to my third observation. *Not only is cultural diversity not new, but the Christian community's ethical awareness of cultural diversity is not new.* As long as there have been Christians, Christian cultural pluralism has been a reality. This fact appears on the pages of the New Testament. I briefly explore it in terms of two specific examples. The first comes from the ministry of Jesus as portrayed by the Gospel of Mark. Jesus, a pious Jew, encounters a Greek women, "a Syro-Phoenician by birth," that is, a foreigner, a woman from a different cultural group. She begs Jesus to exorcize a demon from her daughter. Jesus responds to her:

> "Let the children be fed first. For it is not right to take the food of the children and throw it to the dogs." She replied and said to him, "Lord, even the dogs under the table eat the children's scraps." Then he said to her, "For saying this, you may go. The demon has gone out of your daughter." When the woman went home, she found the child lying in bed and the demon gone. (Mk 8:27-30)

In this peculiar text, Mark puts a claim to cultural privilege on the lips of Jesus, only to have that claim delegitimized in favor of the woman's argument that "even the dogs eat the scraps."[5] Many subversive hermeneutical readings of this text can and have been offered in recent years, both from feminist and post-colonial perspectives, as well as from the viewpoint of ethnicity.[6] I prescind from these in order to highlight a simple point: the tensions that result from cultural diversity and gender difference appear in Jesus' own ministry.[7] Moreover, in this case, the text resolves the tensions in favor of the outsider (symbolized here by the foreign woman). The *other* has a claim on Jesus. As a result, the mission of Jesus is not to be restricted to any culturally privileged group. Likewise, at least in principle, the church as the community of disciples gathered in Jesus' name does not restrict access to Jesus according to culturally exclusionary criteria.

If the New Testament teaches as a basic lesson that cultural *identity* should not determine one's suitability for membership in the Christian community, a further implication has to do with the fundamental inclusiveness of the Christian *mission*. This theme shines through the Pentecost narrative at the beginning of the Acts of the Apostles.

> Now there were devout Jews from every nation under heaven staying in Jerusalem. At the sound [of the driving wind], they gathered in a large crowd, but they were confused because each one heard [the eleven] speaking in his own language. . . . "We are Parthians, Medes, and Elamites, inhabitants of Mesopotamia, Judea and Cappadocia, Pontus and Asia, Phrygia and Pamphylia, Egypt and the districts of Libya near Cyrene, as well as travelers from Rome, both Jews and

converts to Judaism, Cretans and Arabs, yet we hear them speaking
in our own tongues of the mighty acts of God." (Acts 2:5–6, 7a–10)

Many traditional readings of this account see in it the reversal of the
"curse" of Babel (Gen 11:1–9), where God confused the languages of
the people building the tower of Babel to punish their arrogance. But
many Christian commentators, from the Fathers of the church to modern exegetes and theologians, have also noted that the Pentecost narrative does not present a neat contrast with the story of Babel.[8] The gift
of the Spirit does not result in the return to a single language. Luke takes
pains to be clear on this point: the plurality, the diversity, and even the
strangeness of the various languages (cultures) are preserved and utilized
by the Spirit. Old divisions are overcome, not by imposing a single language and culture, but through a genuine sensitivity to and appreciation
of diverse languages and cultures. Luke goes on to testify that some three
thousand new believers were added to their number. We have here not
only the baptism of the three thousand, but also, it appears, the embrace
of their cultural diversity.

Summarizing these first three points, (1) as far as we can tell the diversity of cultures dates to the dawn of the human race. (2) As an historical reality it embraces all of us. Moreover, (3) the Christian tradition
has consistently acknowledged cultural diversity and, building on the
traditions of Israel, the church has insisted on the dignity of the other
and the importance of building up a Christian unity that recognizes and
celebrates difference. Hence, both in the American experience and
throughout its entire history, the church has been aware of cultural diversity and of its call to engage diverse cultures in its evangelical mission.
At least to some extent, ecclesial sensitivity to the ethical implications of
cultural diversity has always been part of the Christian ideal, despite the
fact that the actual historical practice of Christians has often blatantly
contradicted and disfigured it. But I have called cultural diversity a "sign
of the times," a designation that pushes the matter further. This brings
me to my fourth introductory observation.

The demand of diverse cultures for recognition and equality is new. In an
important essay entitled "The Politics of Recognition," Canadian
philosopher Charles Taylor traces some of the developments and tensions that gave birth to the need for a new language and politics of cultural diversity. He begins with an analysis of the modern need and demand for recognition which both individuals and groups experience. "A
number of strands in contemporary politics turn on the need, sometimes

the demand, for *recognition*. The need, it can be argued, is one of the driving forces behind nationalist movements in politics. And the demand comes to the fore in a number of ways in today's politics, on behalf of minority or 'subaltern' groups, in some forms of feminism and in what is today called the politics of 'multiculturalism.'"⁹

Taylor's remarks indicate that what is "new" about cultural diversity emerged alongside a new historical consciousness, a rising sense of the historicity of culture itself and of every culture, and new political, economic, and legal insights into cultural complexity and its implications. What is new also finds expression in contemporary literature and philosophy. It has required the development of new categories to conceptualize the reality of cultural differences so as to avoid diluting that reality through the uncritical use of abstractly universal terms. It takes shape sociologically, both in the genesis of the social sciences themselves, and in the social realities which the term "culture" denotes.

Thus, while patriarchal oppression is ancient, feminist, womanist, and *mujerista,* consciousness of that oppression has emerged fairly recently. While the marginalization of people with disabilities is not new, real awareness of the cultures of disability and the dynamics of those cultures and their demands are new. Nor is discrimination based on sexual identity new (even if such discrimination manifests particularly virulent forms under the aegis of modernity); what is new is the realization that we cannot understand the reality of sexual preference apart from the cultures that express or repress it. As each of these examples suggests, the new attention to cultural diversity involves the humbling acknowledgment that we cannot access the significance of such diversity apart from a genuine encounter with members of diverse cultures.

The new awareness of cultural diversity has emerged as part of a much larger current in the history of ideas and cultural movements, and above all in relation to the historical realities of multiple concrete encounters among peoples of diverse cultures. The realities are not new, but a new awareness of them as realities, the appearance of emancipative movements connected with this awareness and, in recent decades, the emergence of theologies of liberation linked to these emancipative impulses, have eloquently witnessed to the fact that we have entered a new period. How might we characterize this new awareness of diverse cultures and our new theological evaluation of cultural diversity? In the past, theologians may have been aware of the *fact* of diverse cultures, but cultural diversity—and, even more significantly, diverse cultures—did not operate as *theological terms.* Hence, the commonplace awareness of the existence of diverse cultures carries with it a theological density that has gone unnoticed until now.

Herein lies the reason why I characterize cultural diversity as a sign of the times. Cultural realities and differences influence theological interpretations of the faith. It is not the bare fact of cultural diversity, nor even the ethical imperative to act justly toward other cultures, that crafts a distinctively revelatory moment from the dawning awareness of cultural pluralism. It is the further realization that cultures shape persons by producing the symbols without which self-expression would be impossible. Insofar as persons are the recipients of God's saving self-communication, culture plays an irreducible role in salvation. Insofar as culturally conditioned sacramental symbols mediate grace, culture plays an irreducible role in the transmission of God's grace. These insights give rise to the theological imperative to think about faith in the light of culture and to think about the church in the light of the newly emergent significance of every culture.

CULTURAL DIVERSITY
AS DANGEROUS MEMORY

Up to this point I have dropped hints that, in terms of genuinely engaging cultural diversity in the ways we think and live as a church, we have only scratched the surface. Now it is time to go beyond the hints. What I propose to do in this second section can be summarized as a resolution: that we move from the somewhat familiar but abstract awareness of cultural diversity in our church, to a deeply felt engagement with diverse cultures in the very dynamics of church life and subsequently in theological reflection on church life. I begin with what I consider the central affirmation of this chapter. *Cultural diversity is not just about diversity: it is also about racism and discrimination, domination and oppression, exploitation and impoverishment.* I name here three broad aspects of our social life: sociality, politics, and economics. Who belongs? Who wields the power? Who are the owners? Other aspects could be detailed, but this way of schematizing our historical reality confronts us with the main issues at the heart of cultural diversity.

My point here is uncomplicated. Cultural diversity refers not only to a *quantitative* reality, the sheer multiplicity of different groups, but to the theologically significant *qualitative* dynamics of the relationships among those groups. In order to arrive at a genuine theological attentiveness to the significance of cultural diversity, we need to begin with a qualitatively new awareness of the dynamics of racial and cultural discrimination, economic oppression, and political injustice. Moreover, we cannot cultivate a genuine theological awareness of cultural diversity without remembering how we arrived at where we are.

I made reference above to the task of remembering. I return to this point in the present context and propose that the experiences of diverse cultures are encoded in their "dangerous memories." I borrow the notion of dangerous memory from the German theologian Johann Baptist Metz, who employs it as a primary anthropological category for fundamental theology:

> There are some very different kinds of memories. There are those in which we just do not take the past seriously enough: memories in which the past becomes a paradise without danger, a refuge from our present disappointments—the memory of the "good old days.". . . Here the past is filtered through a harmless cliché: everything dangerous, oppressive and demanding has vanished from it: it seems deprived of all future. In this way, memory can easily become a "false consciousness" of our past and an opiate for our present. But there is another form of memory: there are dangerous memories, memories that make demands on us. There are memories in which earlier experiences break through to the center point of our lives and reveal new and dangerous insights for the present. They illuminate for a few moments and with a harsh steady light the questionable nature of things we have apparently come to terms with, and show up the banality of our supposed "realism." They break through the canon of all that is taken as self-evident, and unmask as deception the certainty of those "whose hour is always there" (Jn 7:6). They seem to subvert our structures of plausibility. Such memories are like dangerous and incalculable visitants from the past. They are memories we have to take into account; memories, as it were, with a future content.[10]

The importance of Metz's distinction for Christian theology can hardly be overstated. He developed these insights through conversations with Jews, in his engagement with Jewish thought, and above all by directly confronting the fearsome reality of Auschwitz. Auschwitz stands as a quintessential example of dangerous memory, the kind of memory capable of mediating a genuine future. Metz links this example to another dangerous memory, the primordial dangerous memory for Christians: the *memoria passionis, mortis, et resurrectionis Jesu Christi*.[11] This subversive memory and the scandal embedded in it lie at the very heart of the sacramental tradition that repeats Jesus' words, "do this in remembrance of me." These words bid us to take up Jesus' dangerous proclamation of God's subversive Reign, and to act as he did in solidarity with those whom our world despises and ignores. This foundational, sacramental affirmation indicates that we find, affirm, and embody our very identity as Christians in the dangerous memory of Jesus.

Cultural memory serves as the ground beneath a people. It bestows meaning and content on the names of children. Likewise, the recovery of memory often serves as the key that unlocks and opens the future. Recent efforts to recover historical memory in countries like South Africa and Guatemala give testimony to this point. They also witness to the risk and the danger involved.[12] The history of the United States provides numerous dramatic examples of how memory gets suppressed or erased, and why its dangerous sting gets drawn. Let me cite one seemingly innocuous example of the difference between a nostalgic exercise of memory and what Metz calls dangerous memory. Recently, the news media reported that the owners of the legal rights to the famous novel and movie *Gone With the Wind* had filed a lawsuit to block the publication by Alice Randall of her new book, *The Wind Done Gone*, which examines the realities portrayed in the original book from a new perspective, that of the black slaves.[13] Nearly a century and a half after the Emancipation Proclamation, this legal dispute is replicating the very logic surrounding the issue of slavery itself. Is the story someone's property, an economic right to be protected with all the force of the law? Or is the story someone's life, someone's soul, someone's future? The way we remember the historical realities in question shapes the way we answer these questions.

My own story bristles with danger. The questions we never asked as children! How did the Mexican men who worked on our Wyoming sheep ranch manage to live on six dollars a day? Was that enough? More importantly, who were they? Where were their homes? Were they married? If so, who and where were their wives? Did they have children? And did those children ever get to see their fathers? There were other dangerous issues related to this one. I wanted to study Spanish in high school, but my parents discouraged me from doing so because Spanish was a language only lower-class peoples spoke. They wanted me to learn a cultured tongue, so I studied Latin. My spontaneous desires defied taboos I could not see and abraded sensibilities I did not understand until years later.

A different example emerges from the archives of my home state, which preserves but also effectively covers up some of its most important and dangerous historical memories. Only as an adult did I learn about the massacre that occurred in 1885, in Rock Springs, a dusty little town on the Union Pacific railroad in southern Wyoming. A racially motivated riot led to the brutal massacre of twenty-eight Chinese immigrants who had helped build the railroad and were now working for a coal-mining company. The homes of seventy-nine Chinese families were burned to the ground. More than 550 workers and their wives and children, people of Chinese ancestry, abandoned the Wyoming Territory forever. Very few Asian Americans live in the state of Wyoming today.

The most dangerous memory of all emerged with the most innocent of questions. Where did arrowheads come from? I remember how, when herding sheep, my younger brothers and I loved to tramp around a certain spot on the Thirty-Three Mile Stock Trail outside of Casper hunting for arrowheads. The First People to live in that place, the Arapaho, used to camp near that very spot. Naturally, they were not herding sheep to the Bighorn Mountains. They were hunting buffalo. But only years later, as a young man who had just entered the Jesuit novitiate, did I begin to ask unsettling questions about that place. It started with a book, Dee Brown's *Bury My Heart at Wounded Knee*, whose dangerous memories raised up a disturbing realization. The place where I had grown up, a part of my very bones and blood, had been the place of another people. These wide-open spaces—our ranch, my home, the land my family owned—were stolen. The people of the land had been annihilated. As a child I experienced the Bighorns as a sacred place. I cannot visit now without hearing a low moan carried on the wind, the cry of a people who are no more, whose names have vanished, whose stories only the arrowheads tell. I had stumbled onto a dangerous memory and it changed me. It interrogated me and required me to ask, who are my people and what had we done?

Finally, I need to add that joining the Jesuits did not let me off the hook. I spent a number of years, beginning in novitiate and continuing through my formation, learning about the Society of Jesus. I reflected on the faith that does justice, read about heroic forerunners like Ignatius Loyola, Francis Xavier, and Peter Claver, and pondered the wisdom and witness of great contemporaries like Pedro Arrupe, Karl Rahner, Alfred Delp, and Rutilio Grande. But it was years later, well over a decade after I had entered the Society of Jesus, that I discovered one of our most sordid community secrets. From early in the eighteenth century until 1838, the Jesuits of the Maryland mission, the founders of Georgetown University, owned slaves.[14] My Jesuit brothers justified this sinful practice with spurious racist reasoning, enforced it through the use of the usual corporal punishments, and finally ended it not by freeing the slaves, but by selling them to the former governor of Louisiana. Why didn't we learn about this in our first course in the history of the Society of Jesus? What does it say about us that we have allowed this dangerous memory to fade? And what have we done as a religious body to make restitution for this terrible exploitation of human labor, this affront to human dignity?

Finally, it is important to note that memories like these do not only belong to the distant past. Consider the following news items culled from the last decade in the United States, including my home state of Wyoming.

> A twenty-five-year-old black man, Rodney G. King, is beaten by 21 Los Angeles City police officers—he is left with a split inner lip, a partially paralyzed face, nine skull fractures, a broken cheek bone, a shattered eye socket, and a broken leg. James Byrd, a black man, is dragged to death behind a truck in a small Texas town by a group of young white men, at least one of whom knew Byrd. Haitian immigrant Abner Louima is so brutally beaten by police that he requires hospitalization and surgery. Amadou Diallo, an unarmed African immigrant man is shot 41 times as he reaches for his wallet. In the course of twelve months, 15 black men are fatally shot by Cincinnati police. A white gunman with a hate psychosis fires an automatic weapon at a day-care center for Jewish toddlers, then kills an Asian American postal carrier. Matthew Shepherd, a slightly-built homosexual college student, is brutally beaten and left tied to a fence to die near Laramie, Wyoming.[15]

All memories, all stories of the past, raise questions, but dangerous memories spawn disturbing questions. When did the European immigrant church slip into the patterns of a racist, dominant class? Why did my particular ethnic group and my religious community become part of the White supremacist majority in the United States?[16] How did my family, descended from immigrants and themselves victims of discrimination, end up looking down on the languages and experiences of "lower-class peoples"? What can I as an individual and we as a church do about it now?[17] In posing these disturbing questions, I intend no disrespect to my parents, my state, my nation, or my religious community. I raise these questions not out of disrespect but out of respect—respect for the victims of slavery, exploitation, and conquest, a respect that considers the truth about family, nation, and church in the light cast by dangerous memories.

Engaging people of diverse cultures puts us in touch with their dangerous memories, memories of suffering, discrimination, political exclusion, and impoverishment. Likewise, it raises questions about our own complicity in those experiences of suffering. But the need to admit dangerous questions into consciousness often appears in tandem with a temptation to get through them quickly, to smooth over the painful chapters of the stories, to devise explanations that "let us off the hook." In other words, the challenge of encountering diverse cultures can be subtly co-opted. It thus helps to distinguish between a *cheap recognition of cultural diversity* and a *costly recognition of cultural diversity*, to paraphrase Dietrich Bonhoeffer. The former pays lip service to political correctness. The dominant group honors the cultures of non-dominant groups but surrenders none of its cultural hegemony or privilege. In effect, the representatives of minority groups are employed to embellish public rituals, or a few people of color are given visible, superficial roles in the structures of power, but no real power. Meanwhile, the major media organizations approach the past in a haze of nostalgia, distorting the connections between the suffering of some and the privilege of others, and the predominantly White economic elites disavow any present responsibility for the violent inequalities that exist among diverse cultural groups.

By contrast, a costly recognition of cultural diversity, like Bonhoeffer's "costly grace," moves us beyond the surface level of image manipulation and political gamesmanship, into the realm where our deepest human identities and destinies are forged. This move requires a new willingness on our part as Christians to examine our collective conscience. We cannot embrace cultural diversity if we do not confront the structural, dialectically related realities of privilege and want, the logic of power, and the dynamics of cultural supremacy, as well as the systemic, often implicit attitudes and behaviors associated with these. Embracing cultural diversity interrupts all overt and covert attempts to cover up the realities of racism, economic exploitation, and political domination on the part of a historically dominant group. It entails discovering the connections between our behaviors as a dominant group and the effects of our behaviors on the victims of cultural hegemony.

The costly recognition of cultural diversity accepts that racism and discrimination, domination and oppression, exploitation and impoverishment, are dialectically related to one another. The flip side of poverty is privilege and, like poverty, privilege has a history. It is not only a history of discovery, hard work, and good luck, but of conquest, exploitation, and rigged scales. Likewise, every incident of racial or sexual discrimination involves people who are racists or sexists. Our political system, with its carefully regulated borders, produces people who can act and others who cannot, people who wield power and others who do not, people who are somebodies and others discarded as nobodies. These oppositions are neither accidental nor coincidental. They create one another. Moreover, inside this cruel dialectic, individual people and whole peoples vanish. Their names, languages, and stories disappear from memory. Here lies the hidden moral scandal beneath unacknowledged economic privilege and cultural supremacy.

To acknowledge this scandal deepens the encounter with those who suffer its violence. It frees us to listen to their memories of suffering, to honor their legitimate hopes, and to pray for their deepest aspirations, even when listening, honoring, and praying exposes the underside of our own stories. Likewise, authentic engagement with other cultures calls forth action. It does not stop with the knowledge of their dangerous memories of discrimination, oppression, and impoverishment. It confronts, critiques, and acts against racism, domination, and exploitation, including our own. A Gospel-oriented response to cultural diversity springs from a Gospel-nurtured discipleship willing to read and embrace that diversity as a sign of the times.

CULTURAL DIVERSITY
AS GIFT TO THEOLOGY

In view of the preceding section, it might appear strange to speak of cultural diversity as a *gift*. What I have just described appears more like an *affliction*. However, the same biblical logic that paradoxically exalts "negative" terms such as desert, exile, and cross comes into play here. In the words of Metz quoted at the beginning of this chapter, the encounter with diverse cultures wounds our "preformulated certainties." For this very reason we can once again "talk about God in Jesus' sense." The dangerous memories latent in cultural diversity interrupt our normal routines and evict us from our comfortable lives; insofar as they facilitate a conversion, a return to our fundamental identity as followers of Jesus Christ, they represent a *gift*. Likewise, the costly encounter with diverse cultures discredits every version of the Jesus story that leaves "outsiders" on the outside. Hence, it offers a specific gift to *theology* insofar as it confronts abstract theological methods and ahistorical theological affirmations.

The encounter with diverse cultures is one of many historical signs that impel theology to become a theology of the signs of the times. For Catholic theology, this invitation was given voice by the Second Vatican Council in its Constitution on the Church in the Modern World (*Gaudium et Spes*). But what does it entail? The content of the phrase "a theology of the signs of the times" can be read in two different ways, as Jon Sobrino notes:

> This dialectic between past and present in revelation is what, dogmatically and pastorally, is at stake for theology in reading the "signs of the times." As we know, the constitution *Gaudium et Spes* speaks of the "signs of the times" as events and tendencies that characterize an age (no. 4)—signs of the times in a *historical-pastoral* sense. But this is not the deepest meaning of the expression, even though theology seems to use only this sense. In effect, the same constitution refers to authentic signs of God's presence and purpose" (no. 11)—signs of the times in a sense we can call *historical-theological*. If one takes this seriously, it means that God is still manifesting himself today.[18]

Sobrino suggests that both meanings of the phrase "signs of the times" are valid and necessary. However, he stresses the latter meaning, both because we tend to overlook it and, more importantly, because it involves something like a revolution in the way we understand faith, church, and theology. If signs of the times such as cultural diversity function as theological terms for revelatory realities, then a theology attuned to read them puts the community of faith in touch with God's gratuitous presence in new and powerful ways. This means that the dangerous and painful memories encoded in the encounter with diverse cultures represent more than an indictment of the heirs of privilege. They point to the place where those same heirs meet God. However, acknowledging this shifts the very criteria for what constitutes authentic religious practice. Among other things, it means theology needs to think about its task in a new way. It needs to actually incarnate itself among different peoples and cultures, and that "dangerous remembering" is part of the very self-definition of theology. That is, in order to speak rightly about God, theology must "take on history." In the process, it discovers that its own deepest insights into transcendent reality are not compromised by history. If anything, they are made more concrete, more accessible, more real. Theology can once again talk about God in Jesus' sense.

A shift occurs in the self-understanding of theology when theology takes on history. Although this shift has many facets, I wish to focus on two. *First, theology does not directly reflect on God, but on the self-communication of God in history.* In the biblical tradition, faith is not abstract but practical. It finds a body not in a set of propositions but in concrete acts of love. Similarly, God's self-communication focuses not on a set of timeless truths but an historical journey. We discover who God is and what God wants by following Jesus. Significantly, God's self-communication is mediated by historical realities, including such signs of the times as the deep recognition of cultural diversity. That is, the community of faith encounters God in and through the diversity of cultures, discovering there an ever deeper sense of its identity and mission. In this way, cultural diversity assumes the status of a theological term. It functions as a revelatory reality. It should be noted that the designation sign of the times does not imply that the revelatory importance of cultural diversity lies directly on the surface. Its implications for the church and its mission cannot be plucked like grapes from the pages of our most recent census report, even though these cannot be apprehended apart from the demographic realities detailed in such reports.

More importantly, this sign of the times cannot be captured in theological *concepts* alone. It emerges as *sign* on the level of *committed faith* in the midst of everyday, real-world *action*. Hence, while the signs of the times reveal transcendent reality, they must be apprehended as historical realities, embraced through historical commitments, and expressed in historical praxis. As reflection, theology finds itself situated in and affected by historical reality. As reflection upon a faith commitment, it sharpens the ethical sensitivities embedded in our commitments. As reflection upon a faith commitment expressed through historical praxis, it broadens the scope and deepens the impact of that praxis. A theology of the signs of the times does not conceive its task in exclusively conceptual terms. Theology not only "thinks" about God, but commits to God's way and acts on God's word. It integrates conceptualization, commitment, and praxis. It treats cultural diversity not only as a pastoral problem to be addressed but as a theological place where believers encounter God's presence and discern God's will.

The second facet is closely linked to the first. *Theology not only reflects on cultural diversity, but opts to remain open to further authentic encounters with diverse cultures.* This option for cultural diversity and pluralism echoes one of the great theological discoveries of our times, the "preferential option for the poor."[19] First articulated by liberation theology and later embraced by official Catholic social teaching, the preferential option for the poor shows theology how to take on history by putting itself in the place where history most clearly reveals its inner logic.[20] Similarly, the option for cultural diversity places theologians where they might not otherwise locate themselves. It does not replace the preferential option for the poor. In fact, it is best understood as complementing it: the option to remain open to authentic encounters with diverse cultures entails a *preferential* openness to the cultures of people who are poor, marginalized, and oppressed. In the context of cultural diversity, a preferential option for the victims of racism, exclusion, and exploitation is precisely what leads to a *costly* encounter with their dangerous memories.[21] Likewise, solidarity with members of marginalized cultures (i.e., the Syro-Phoenician woman) goes to the heart of the church's mission. Such solidarity verifies the church's faithfulness to Jesus' own witness. On the level of action, genuine openness to cultural diversity seeks to establish justice on the earth by uncovering and transforming the social structures that shape historical reality. It exposes and transforms racist structures into structures of acceptance and openness. It converts oppressive and violent structures into structures of justice and peace. Finally, a spirituality of solidarity, marked by the experience of the human sacrament of relationship, discovers in the encounter with diverse cultures a concrete way to be Christian. The very act of entering into solidarity represents a form of evangelization.

What impact does the shift to a theology of the signs of the times have on the ordinary understanding of the Christian faith and, above all, for the ways we think about the church? First of all, a theology of the signs of the times introduces a fundamental and life-giving change into the way we conceive the nature of faith. The fundamental problem for faith does not have to do with gathering a consensus around a set of religious *propositions* believed to be true. The question is not: How do we get everyone to subscribe to the Christian faith and to join the Christian church? Rather, the fundamental problem has to do with finding salvation. The questions we need to ask are these: Where and how and when can we meet the living God? Ignacio Ellacuría articulates the problem this way:

> The problem for faith and, consequently, for theology in our situation today, is a problem with clearly defined features. It does not depend principally on the will of the ecclesiastical hierarchy nor on the pretensions of theologians, but on what is the concrete reality of the people of God. The salvation of God, and the salvific mission of the church and the faith, concretize their universality here and now in

very precise forms. The theologian will have to investigate this, re-flecting in a first moment on the signs in which are revealed and concealed the salvific presence of God in a Jesus who continues be-coming flesh throughout history.[22]

As Ellacuría indicates, the question emerges from the concrete circum-stances of a people in need of salvation. The task of theology is not in the first place to provide conceptual answers to abstract questions. It is to discern in the signs of the times the concrete hunger for salvation and the signs of salvation that concretely meet those hungers.

This shift in the understanding of the nature of faith opens new possibilities for how we think about the church. The church is an his-torical reality in and through which God is present and active. It comes into possession of its own concrete *nature* through the exercise of its *mis-sion*. Moreover, it stays alive in history not by maintaining its structures but by constantly carrying out its mission. For this reason, the church has continually needed to read the signs of the times. Throughout history, it has borrowed social and political forms, along with different ministries and offices, from the various ages and cultures in which it lived. It de-veloped particular ecclesial structures in response to different historical circumstances, and these structures mediated with greater or lesser clar-ity the saving presence of God. Like other social organisms, it developed structures of authority and accountability. But a theological account of ecclesial authority must not be reduced to a juridical view based on ec-clesial offices such as bishop or pope, even though it should not be sep-arated from the offices that developed in order to exercise the "ministry of administration." In view of the signs of the times, the exercise of au-thority seeks truth by theological discernment and depends on human competence. In thinking about each of these important aspects of the church—its nature and mission, its ministries and office, its authority and competence—the church is enriched by every encounter that inclines it to "take on history." In this way, the encounter with cultural diversity concretely liberates and enriches the ways we think about the church.

Encountering diverse cultures invites us to perceive reality and to think about our theological interpretations of reality in new ways. Similarly, *thinking about cultural diversity* opens up the possibility of imagining reli-gious practices and the very nature of the church anew. It changes our understanding of theology and the content of our theology of the church. This in turn influences the ways we act as a church, above all, how we act toward others—those of other faiths and those of other cultures who share our faith. It even influences the ways we act toward people of our own cultures. Thus, this new way of thinking about the church creates space for thinking about new forms and structures of ministry in the church, and new ways to authentically exercise ecclesial authority. If we take a hold of this sign of the times and embrace its gift, we become attuned to other signs of the times. In the many faces, we discover anew that the church, the community shaped by the dangerous memory of Jesus, exists to provide diverse points of contact with the saving presence of God. Finally, the most profound gift mediated by the willingness to authentically engage diverse cultures is this: encountering cultural diversity exposes us to the gratuitous newness of God. In the presence of those who come from many different places, we discover anew the meaning of coming home.

NOTES

1. Johann Baptist Metz, *A Passion for God* (New York/Mahwah, N.J.: Paulist Press, 1998), 2.

2. See Vatican II, *Gaudium et Spes*, nos. 4, 11. Two things should be noted. First, this assumption is not gratuitous, but a detailed argument in its favor goes beyond the limits of this particular investigation. Second, to highlight a "sign of the times" implies a particular stance with regard to the dynamics of divine revelation and the nature of historical reality. As Gustavo Gutiérrez notes, "a theology that begins with the signs of the times is a dynamic reflection, placed at the service of the ecclesial task. It is a theology attentive to the historical moment in which we live." See Gustavo Gutiérrez, *The Density of the Present* (Maryknoll, N.Y.: Orbis Books, 1999), 5–6. I will return to this point later in this chapter. For now, suffice it to say that God's revelation flows to specific peoples in concrete places at particular times and in distinctive ways.

3. Drawing on the thought of Ignacio Ellacuría, I call this approach a "theology of historical reality" or, more expressively, a "theology of the signs of the times." The technical phrase, "historical reality," comes from Ellacuría, who develops it in dialogue with his philosophical mentor, Xavier Zubiri. See Ignacio Ellacuría, *Filosofía de la realidad histórica* (San Salvador: UCA Editores, 1990); "Hacia una fundamentación filosófica del método teológico latinoamericano," *Escritos teológicos* (San Salvador: UCA Editores, 2000), 187–218. See also Kevin F. Burke, *The Ground Beneath the Cross: The Theology of Igncio Ellacuría* (Washington, D.C.: Georgetown University Press, 2000).

4. Jay Dolan, *The American Catholic Experience: A History from Colonial Times to the Present* (Garden City, N.Y.: Double & Company, 1985), 127–28.

5. In Matthew, the basis on which the counter-claim is made is the woman's faith (Mt 15:28).

6. See, for example, Sharon H. Ringe, "A Gentile Woman's Story," in *Feminist Interpretation of the Bible*, ed. Letty Russell (Philadelphia: Westminster Press, 1983), 65–72; Elaine Wainwright, "A Voice from the Margin: Reading Matthew 15:21–28 in an Australian Feminist Key," in *Reading from This Place*, vol. 2, ed. Fernando Segovia and Mary A. Tolbert (Minneapolis: Fortress Press, 1995), 132–53; Kwok Pui-Lan, *Discovering the Bible in the Non-Biblical World* (Maryknoll, N.Y.: Orbis Books, 1995), 71–83; Jim Perkinson, "A Canaanitic Word in the Logos of Christ: Or the Difference the Syro-Phoenician Woman Makes to Jesus," *Semeia* 75 (1996): 61–85; Chad Myers, *Binding the Strong Man: A Political Reading of Mark's Story of Jesus* (Maryknoll, N.Y.: Orbis Books, 1988), 203–05.

7. I am not attempting to comment on the historicity of the events portrayed in this text. Whether or not this encounter occurred within the historical ministry of Jesus, the Gospel writer portrays it as happening in the historical ministry of Jesus, thus giving the tensions implicit in the narrative a certain theological weight.

8. For a contemporary reflection on this point, see Gutiérrez, *The Density of the Present*, 194–201.

9. Charles Taylor, *Multiculturalism and "The Politics of Recognition"* (Princeton, N.J.: Princeton University Press, 1992), 25. I will argue below that this demand for "recognition" needs to be part of the new self-understanding of theology.

10. Johann Baptist Metz, "The Future in the Memory of Suffering," in *Faith and the Future*, ed. Johann Baptist Metz and Jürgen Moltmann, trans. John Griffiths (Maryknoll, N.Y.: Orbis Books, 1995), 7–8.

11. Johann Baptist Metz, *Faith in History and Society* (London: Burns & Oates, 1980), 90.

12. Recall that in 1998, Bishop Juan Girardi, the auxiliary bishop of Guatemala City and the chair of the Guatemalan Bishops' Conference "Recovery of Historical Memory Project" (REMHI), was bludgeoned to death with a piece of cement block two days after the publication of the REMHI report, *Nunca Mas*. For an abridged English translation of that report, see *Guatemala: Never Again!* (Maryknoll, N.Y.: Orbis Books, 1999).

13. See Kenneth N. Gilpin, "Doubt Is Raised on Lawsuits on 'The Wind Done Gone,'" *New York Times,* October 11, 2001; David Kirkpatrick, "Mitchell Estate Settles 'Gone with the Wind' Suit," *New York Times*, May 10, 2002.

14. See the illuminating investigation by Edward F. Beckett, "Listening to Our History: Inculturation and Jesuit Slaveholding," *Studies in the Spirituality of Jesuits* 28, no. 5 (1996).

15 M. Shawn Copeland, "Racism and the Vocation of the Theologian." Address presented at the annual convention of the Catholic Theological Society of America, Milwaukee, Wisconsin, June 8, 2001.

16. It might be important for U.S. Catholics of Irish descent to complement their reading of the well-known book by Thomas Cahill, *How the Irish Saved Civilization,* with the unsettling analysis put forth by Noel Ignatiev, *How the Irish Became White* (New York: Routledge, 1996).

17. For an enlightened and profoundly challenging reflection on the responsibilities of the White U.S. Catholic *theologian* in response to these and similar questions, see Margaret Eletta Guider, "Moral Imagination and the *Missio ad gentes*: Redressing the Counterwitness of Racism," in *Proceedings of the Catholic Theological Society of America,* ed. Richard Sparks (Milwaukee, Wisc., June 7–10, 2001), 49–69.

18. Jon Sobrino, *Christ the Liberator: A View from the Victims,* trans. Paul Burns (Maryknoll, N.Y.: Orbis Books, 2001), 201.

19. In an effort to accommodate the overwhelming complexity at work in the mingling of cultures, I formulate this option in these very broad terms: *to remain open to further authentic encounters with diverse cultures.* In fact, this way of putting it may be overly broad and in need of further refinement. My point here is that *option* must be regarded as an intrinsic element of theology. Authentic readings of the sign of the times do not happen automatically; they happen when theologians place themselves where such signs can be perceived.

20. Ellacuría writes: "The poor of Latin America are theological place insofar as they constitute the maximum and scandalous, prophetic and apocalyptic presence of the Christian God and, consequently, the privileged place of Christian praxis and reflection." See Ignacio Ellacuría, "Los pobres, 'lugar teológico' en America Latina," *Escritos teológicos* 1, 148. See also Jon Sobrino, *Jesus the Liberator,* 23–24.

21. Critics of liberation theology have objected to the language of "preferential" option, and one might expect the same objections to be raised here. But as Gutiérrez explains, far from being exclusive, the preferential option is precisely that which opens us to the universality of God's call and grace: "The God proclaimed by Jesus Christ is the God whose call is universal, addressing every human person, but it is at the same time a God who loves the poor and the dispossessed with a preferential love. This dialectic between universality and particularity is a demand and a challenge to the community of the Lord's disciples." Gutiérrez, *The Density of the Present Moment,* 24–45.

22. Ellacuría, "Hacia una fundamentación filosófica," 212–13.

3

BLACK CATHOLICS IN THE UNITED STATES: A SUBVERSIVE MEMORY

Diana Hayes

Over the course of the past decade I have been speaking about the
coming of the third millennium in a number of different ways, ask-
ing: "What will the church look like; what should it look like? Are these
questions not necessarily the same? What will and what should the theology of the third millennium be? What are the context(s) for doing
theology? What should its emphases, its sources, and its areas of concern
be? What will be the role of persons of color, who now make up the
majority of Catholics globally? How do we Catholics of every race and
nation, of every tongue, of every class, from bishops to laity, bring about
the changes that are needed in our church, and more importantly, what
should these changes be? How will they affect our liturgy, our parishes,
our dioceses, and our lives as faithful and faith-filled Catholics?"

My constant emphasis has been that we must be aware of the demographic shifts which are taking place in our nation and in our church,
shifts that place Latinos/as as the largest group of persons of color in the
United States; that we must listen to and affirm the voices of those marginalized and voiceless, persons of color, women, and far too many others. We need their input for they too are and have always been the
church universal.

The millennium is now here. We are embarking on the third millennium of Christianity throughout the world. The question now is: Was
I heard? Did they hear the voices of Black, Latino/a, Asian, and other
United Statesian theologians who do not fit the historical understanding of who and what a theologian, a leader in our church is? Were we
heard, were we understood, and, most importantly, were we able to make
a difference? In many ways, I believe the answer to that question is yes.

This "Learning Festival" on diversity in the Catholic Church is an example of that "yes."

We who are of African descent and of Roman Catholic faith can, I believe, affirm that changes are taking place, not necessarily as quickly as we would want, perhaps not necessarily in as great a depth or in all of the areas that we have targeted, but yes, changes have indeed taken place. These changes have occurred not simply as the result of a change of heart on the part of the church's hierarchy but because through perseverance and persistence, a sleeping giant has been awakened. That giant is the Black Catholic community, three million strong and still growing in the United States. With our Latino, Asian, Caribbean, and Native American brothers and sisters, we are the new face of the Roman Catholic Church not just in the United States but throughout the world.

What proof do I have of this? The presence of those gathered for this Learning Festival, the young and the not so young, men and women, laity and religious, of various races and genders, all engaged at various levels in the pursuit of theological and other forms of knowledge which will enable them to become the leaders of our church in the future. Equally important are those not present but working just as diligently whom I encounter in my classes, at other conferences, and in parishes throughout the nation.

BLACK CATHOLICS
IN THE UNITED STATES

The Black Catholic bishops of the United States were truly prophetic in 1984 when they issued their first pastoral letter, *What We Have Seen and Heard*.[1] It was issued in recognition of their belief that the Black Catholic community in the U.S. church had come of age, bringing with it the duty, the privilege, and the joy of sharing with others the rich experience of the Word of Life as it has been lived throughout the almost more than 500 years of Black presence in this land. Today, we have thirteen bishops of whom four are heads of dioceses.[2] There are Offices of Black Catholics in almost every diocese and a Secretariat for Black Catholics in the USCCB. Although there are only six systematic theologians at this time (one bishop, one woman religious, two lay women, and two priests), there are others are at various stages of preparation. We have four church historians, three canon lawyers, and numerous religious brothers and sisters and priests (although the numbers as throughout the Church are falling), and many permanent deacons, catechists, Directors of Religious Education, youth ministers, and even a chancellor (Archdiocese of New York), and the like. All of this growth has occurred in the last thirty or so years but the seeds were planted centuries ago. Yet these numbers do not fully reflect the ferment going on in the heart of the Black Catholic community as it gathers regularly in groups large and small to assess its particular situation in the church.

Today, we are witnessing further signs of that coming of age. Black Catholics in the United States are asserting their rightful places in the Roman Catholic Church, nationally and globally, basing their claim for recognition and inclusion on our history in the American Church, which predates the Mayflower, and in Africa since the beginning of the faith. Our persistent faith gives living expression to the Word of Life, which we have received and which we fully embrace. As the Apostle Paul states: "You are no longer strangers and sojourners, but you are fellow citizens with the saints and members of the household of God, built upon the foundation of the apostles and prophets, Christ Jesus himself being the cornerstone, in whom the whole structure is joined together and grows into a holy temple in the Lord; in whom you also are built into it for a dwelling place of God in the Spirit" (Eph 2:19–22).

Strangers and sojourners no longer, African American Catholics no longer "sing the Lord's song in a strange land" (Ps 137:4). Instead we have taken down our harps and converted that strange land into a homeland, one rich with the woven tapestries of our voices, lifted in praise and song; of our spirituality expressed in deep and heartfelt prayer and preaching; and of our cultural heritage, a rich and colorful mixture of peoples of Africa, the Caribbean, the West Indies, South America, and North America.

Evidence of this newfound land can be seen throughout the United States today in dioceses large and small, rural, urban and suburban, all blessed and invigorated by the presence and spirit of Black Catholics who are busy about the work of Jesus Christ. We are seeking, in Jesus' name, to preach good news to the poor, to proclaim release to the captives, and recovery of sight to the blind, to set at liberty those who are oppressed, to proclaim the acceptable year of the Lord (Lk 4:18–19). For in our holistic worldview, we recognize that life is necessarily interconnected; the sacred and the secular, the workplace and the church, are all imbued with the spirit of God and thus are the responsibility of people of faith at work in God's vineyard.

BLACK CATHOLICS
AND "SUBVERSIVE MEMORY"

Johann Baptist Metz, a German Catholic political theologian, speaks of a "subversive memory" as one which challenges the accepted reality, bringing forth a new understanding, controversial perhaps, but also more truth-filled.[3] The life, death, and resurrection of Jesus Christ is the ultimate "subversive memory" for Christians because it is a memory of life brought forth from death, of good triumphing over evil, the weak over the strong.[4] It is a truth reflected in Mary's magnificent song which proclaims the coming forth of a new way of life, a more just and equitable one (Lk 1:47–55). It is also the nucleus of Jesus' own teaching, especially his first sermon in which he proclaimed the year of jubilee for all who believe (Lk 4:18–19).

The continued presence of Black Catholics in the Catholic Church in the United States serves also as a "subversive memory," one which turns all of reality upside down, for it is a memory of hope brought forth from pain, of perseverance in the face of bloody opposition, of faith born of tortured struggle. It is a dangerous memory, as Kevin Burke notes, for it is the memory of a people required to bring forth life from conditions conducive only to death, again much as Christ himself was restored to life after a scandalous death. Ours is a memory of survival against all odds. It is a memory of a people, born in a strange and too often hostile land, paradoxically celebrating Christ's victory over death as a sign of God's promise of our own eventual liberation from a harsh servitude imposed by our fellow Christians. Today, Black Catholics affirm that we are no longer strangers or sojourners in the Catholic Church in the United States.[5] Our particular historical experience helps to define us and establishes the context from within which we speak about and live out our faith. We must, therefore, also acknowledge the church's painful history in the Americas and the role it played in the development, expansion, and persistence of a particularly horrific form of slavery.

Papal and other official church documents reveal that role. In his *Dum Diversis* of 1452, Nicholas V granted the kings of Spain and Portugal "with our Apostolic Authority, full and free permission to invade, search out, capture and subjugate the Saracens, and pagans and any other unbelievers and enemies of Christ wherever they may be and to reduce their persons into perpetual slavery."[6] Alexander VI extended this permission from Africa to the Americas in 1493. In 1866, the Holy Office stated that "slavery itself is not at all contrary to the natural and divine law."[7] And later, similar statements were issued, despite others which sought to soften their harshness. This enabled many U.S. bishops to ignore the humanity of those enslaved and to deny the human dignity which is given them by a just and loving God. It was not until the Second Vatican Council (1962–1965) that an unequivocal statement against slavery, among other violations of the "integrity of the human person" and insults to human dignity, was finally promulgated (*Gaudium et Spes*, no. 29).

Only in 2002 did John Paul II publicly acknowledge and apologize on behalf of the church universal for its role in the implementation and perpetuation of the slave trade. Although not explicitly acknowledged as such, the emergence and perpetuation of a virulent form of racism which, as noted in 1989 by the Pontifical Commission on Peace and Justice, still persists throughout the world, can arguably be traced back to these pontifical statements and the actions arising from them.[8]

Racism is a fact of life that continues to torment Black Americans regardless of their particular faith. It has its roots in the very foundations of our society and, sadly, in its Judeo-Christian ethic. In drafting the Constitution, the enslavement of Blacks was recognized and accepted. The revolutionary phrases of the Founding Fathers' declaration, proclaiming liberty and justice for all and affirming the equality of all men, ignored the condition of Black humanity. As the late Supreme Court Justice Thurgood Marshall noted, the famous first three words of that document, "We the People," did not include women who were denied the vote and Blacks who were enslaved. The intent was clearly expressed in the notification that Blacks counted as only three-fifths of a white person and then only for the purpose of white male representation in the new Congress. The Constitution was developed not as a color-blind document but as one assuring the domination of White, propertied males over all others living in the newly formed union.[9]

Racism has changed its face, however. Rather than the blatant and overt racism of past years, today we are confronted with a more sinister, because less visible, form of covert or hidden racism manifested particularly as institutional racism. This form of racism "originates in the operation of established and respected forces in the society and thus receives far less public consideration."[10] As such, institutional racism is more than a form sanctioned by the Constitution and laws of a country, as the Vatican Commission suggests. For even after that Constitution has been expunged of its color-bias and the laws mandating segregation and second-class citizenship have been removed, institutionalized racism still persists.

It persists in the very warp and woof of this society, which has, for so long, been imbued with an ideology supported all too often by an erroneous interpretation of the teachings of Sacred Scripture.

Today despite significant changes in the laws governing American society with regard to African Americans, we have reached somewhat of an impasse. Many of those changes are being nullified and labeled as preferential treatment and/or reverse discrimination, somehow ignoring the centuries of slavery and second-class citizenship which has hindered the descendants of African slaves from attaining equal opportunity before the law. It seems peculiarly ironic if not malicious to label as "lazy" welfare queens, women (and their men and children) who have consistently had to struggle for almost five hundred years first as unpaid slaves, then as underpaid sharecroppers, domestics, and factory workers, and today as minimum wage workers, always with little or no meaningful education and certainly little incentive to persevere. Yet somehow they did persevere; they survived and thus serve as a subversive memory for all of America for its failure to live up to its vaunted proclamations and to the church for its denial of their co-creation by a righteous God.

Racism still persists. It is a mind-set which flies in the face of Sacred Scripture and the teachings of the Christian Church. It is a distortion of the teachings that all are endowed with a rational soul and are created in God's own image (*Gaudium et Spes*, no. 29). Racism is incompatible with God's design. It is a sin that goes beyond the individual acts of individual human beings. Racism, to be blunt, is a sin that is incorporated into and becomes a constituent part of the framework of society in which it is the concentration of the personal sins of those who condone this evil.

As stated above, when acknowledging the persistence of racism both in church and world, we must also recognize the role of Christianity not just in perpetuating various forms of racism and ethnocentrism throughout the world but also its role in developing it. Racism did not emerge full-blown from the mind of some individual; rather it is the result of a pattern of behavior which rationalizes the superiority of one group over another. The latter are considered inferior and deserving of being dehumanized or denied basic human and civil rights, by reason of birth, skin color, economic status, religion, language, or some other factor over which they usually have no control.

We too often today seek to deny responsibility for our actions whatever they might be. I have a five-year-old nephew who, when confronted with something he has done or failed to do, immediately says it is the fault of one of his cousins or anyone else but him. What may be harmless defensiveness in a child, especially if confronted and dealt with, cannot be condoned in adults, especially those responsible for the lives of others. Yet we find politicians, educators, CEOs, parents, and too many others in leadership roles denying their responsibility for a failure to act or an act which has had a devastating impact on those caught in their tangled web of deceit.

Hence I rejoice in the fact that the Holy Father, in the Year of Jubilee 2000, apologized for the failures and actions of the church which have caused and continue to cause great harm and pain to many men, women, and children. Many U.S. bishops have done the same. This is a positive step forward but one which must now lead to action beyond just words.[11] Serious efforts must be made to change how persons of color, women, and others are seen and treated, again both in our church and in our society. When the church itself opens its doors to the leadership of all of the faithful in ways that affirm their cultural and ethnic differences while affirming their oneness in faith, we will truly be on the path of reconciliation and healing.

FIVE ISSUES

I was involved for a number of years in the preparations for the eighth National Black Catholic Congress that took place in August 2002 in Chicago, Illinois. This congress, which takes place every five years, has its origins in the five congresses initiated and held by Black Catholic laity (there was only one priest and one unacknowledged Black bishop at that time) in the last decade of the nineteenth century.[12] Interestingly, many of the issues and concerns raised then are still being raised more than a hundred years later. As part of the preparation, I and other Black Catholic scholars traveled the length and breadth of the United States, speaking and listening to Black Catholics at every level of the church about their issues and concerns. I would like to discuss five of them.

First, there is the question of authenticity. Repeatedly, Black Catholics have to prove the legitimacy of their presence within the Roman Catholic Church as a distinct group with a history, culture, and traditions worthy not only of being preserved but also of being shared with the Church as a whole.

Second, many Black Catholics are ignorant of their own history, both in the church and in this country, and many Catholics are uninformed about the rich and diverse history of the Roman Catholic Church throughout the world.

Third, a gap often exists in the understanding and practice of Catholicism among different age groups, even within the same culture. There is also a parochialism which too often restrains Blacks, as well as other Catholics, from evangelizing those around them. I will address this issue in the most detail for in my judgment it is one that impacts all of us greatly.

Fourth, there is the lack of sensitivity and cultural and historical training on the part of priests, religious, deacons, and seminarians who are sent not only into the Black Catholic community but also into any Catholic parish where there are increasing numbers of Black Catholics or other persons of color.

Fifth, there is isolation and its attendant difficulties, when a parish finds itself isolated to a certain extent, in a non-Catholic neighborhood, especially when those living around the church are poor and Black.

The Question of Authenticity

The question of authenticity refers to the perennial burden placed on Catholics of African descent to prove not only their authenticity as Roman Catholics but also their worthiness to be "allowed" to participate in the sacraments and activities of the Church, as if they were newcomers or children. They have to show that they can celebrate their faith in a style and manner in keeping with their culture and heritage.

The late Sr. Thea Bowman proclaimed, as did the Black bishops, that Black Catholic faith is holistic, life-affirming, and community-sustaining. Our spirituality emerges from our African roots without a separation between the sacred and the secular, the individual and the community. It is biblically centered, but Sacred Scripture is not accepted uncritically.[13] Our experience in slavery taught us to read the Bible through the lens of our experience and to proclaim God's word in light of that experience. Unmoved by the diluted and distorted Christianity passed down to us, we have claimed the fullness of God's liberating message as expressed in the person of Jesus Christ the Liberator. God as Creator and Jesus as Liberator are seen as present and active in our lives and as the transcendent source of our lives and our salvation. Black Catholics believe that the Holy Spirit was sent to heal, to nurture, and to sustain us as we wandered in our pilgrimage toward God. God is truly a God who brought us through the "weary years" of slavery and segregation to a time of progress and renewed hope.

We bring a more inclusive understanding of church, one which is open to all of God's people, as it manifests itself in a healing and holy sacramentality, an extension of the Lord's table. Our liturgies invite Catholics from every walk of life, race, class, and gender to make "a joyful noise unto the Lord" in congregations representative of the entire people of God in all their diversity.

Black Catholics also speak a new and challenging word about Mary, the Mother of God, rejecting the symbol of passivity for the courageous and outrageous authority of a young unwed mother who had the faith in herself and in her God to break through the limitations her society placed upon her to say a powerful "yes" to God, standing alone yet empowered. Hers was not a "yes" to being used merely as a passive, empty vessel but a "yes" to empowerment, challenging the status quo by her ability to overcome those who doubted and denied her ability to bring forth and nurture her son as a woman of faith and conviction. The image of Mary and the infant Jesus is one of strength and courage, of a mother's determination to bring forth this child regardless of the opposing circumstances and conditions, a situation in which many Black women have often found themselves.

But why is this "proof" or authentication so often necessary? Historically, persons of African descent have not been seen as Catholic. Despite our over five hundred years in the Church in the United States and our two-thousand-year-old presence in the Universal Church, whose origins were in the Middle East and Africa, including Black Africa, we are usually seen as newcomers, converts all, with little right or authority to demand what is called the "privileges" of the faith.

Ignorance of Many Black Catholics of Their Own History

Historian Cyprian Davis notes:

> Long before Christianity arrived in the Scandinavian countries, at least a century before St. Patrick evangelized Ireland, and over two centuries before St. Augustine would arrive in Canterbury, and almost seven centuries before the conversion of the Poles and the establishment of the kingdom of Poland, this mountainous black kingdom (Ethiopia) was a Catholic nation with its own liturgy, its own spectacular religious art, its own monastic tradition, its saints and its own spirituality.[14]

There has been a peculiar failure of education by the church, one that has only recently been recognized and addressed by the bishops of the United States. Their recent document, *Our Hearts Were Burning Within Us*,[15] on the religious formation of adult Catholics comes at a critical moment in the life of the church today. Against the temptations of an increasingly secular and materialistic society, the document addresses the lack of religious knowledge of many adult Catholics for whom religious education has often ended with their Confirmation. Many never read another thing about church history or doctrine nor have there been many resources for them if they were interested in doing so. As a result, they have been left with a child's faith, although they are mature adults. At the same time, however, the history taught them was inaccurate, Eurocentric in content, with little recognition given to the fact that for its first eight hundred years, the church was predominantly a church of the Middle East and Africa whose cultures influenced its teachings, traditions, liturgy, and very lifestyle.

Nor have we been taught the complete history of the Catholic Church in the United States as most of the emphasis has been on the English-speaking colonies. Consequently, little is known of the Spanish- and French-speaking churches, dating back to this country's earliest beginnings in the sixteenth century, with their rich and diverse histories and the presence of African Catholics who participated both as free men and women and as slaves. Even among the English-speaking colonies, little attention is given to Maryland, the first colony settled by Catholics, and the Black presence there is again ignored. Yet these groups are the oldest continuous line of Catholics in the United States today.[1]

How can we evangelize those who are increasingly unchurched if we fail to catechize those who are churched? We must be able to speak about our faith, what we believe and why, who we are as Catholics, and who we are as children of a loving God, as we ourselves have lived and experienced that faith. This faith does not come naked but is continuously presented and passed on, nurtured and sustained, by the particular peoples who have significance in our lives, who clothe it with cultures, histories, and traditions which have shaped us into the adults that we are today. If we are not open to learning about cultures and peoples unlike us, if we are unwilling to learn the history of the church in all of its diversity, we are doomed to failure before we even begin.

We cannot teach to others what we ourselves do not know. Nor can we lay the burden of responsibility solely on the clergy and/or religious for, as we very well know, many are not of African descent and are in need of further education and conscious-raising, an issue to which I will return.

The Growing Gap between the Young and the Old Generations of the Same or Different Cultures

What is of critical importance about the U.S. bishops' recent pastoral letter *Our Hearts Are Burning Within Us* is that the bishops recognize the need for a continuous formation in the faith that begins in infancy and is ongoing and never-ending. It is critical because those whom we are losing in the church are quite often our young adults who, whether confirmed or not, have reached a time in their lives when they question everything.[17] Too often, the church has not had answers, at least none these young ones are willing or able to hear. As a result, they, as the saying goes, vote with their feet, leaving the Catholic church for other Christian churches, especially non-denominational mega-churches, for Islam, for African traditional religions, or worst of all, for no religion at all. They are swallowed up by lifestyles which are increasingly individualistic, hedonistic, materialistic, and atheistic despite the constant assertions of faith by leading figures in the worlds of sports, entertainment, politics, and business who constantly give "honor" to God while too often blaspheming and dishonoring that same God by their actual behaviors and products.

What of our young people? In many ways, their questions are no different from any of ours and the issue under consideration certainly applies across racial/ethnic lines in the church.

The church, as presently constituted, is often seen as alien to our young people whose eyes are focused on rap, hip-hop, and the media and sports stars of today rather than on the face of Jesus Christ. They are not interested in a God that is impersonal, removed, unmoved, and judgmental. They do not want to be a part of a church that behaves toward them like a rigid, disapproving parent who sees only their faults rather than their dreams and never praises them. They have experienced too much negativity in their short lives, the break-up of their families; the violence in their homes, streets, and schools; the deaths of too many friends; and the constant challenge of simply making it through another day. They seek a God who is personal to them with whom they can share their doubts and fears as well as their hopes and dreams. They are surrounded at every moment of their lives by enticements to indulge themselves in every way possible, without worrying about the consequences, physical, psychological, or moral, for themselves or others. They are looking for someone to guide and advise them but at the same time allow them the opportunity to dialogue, raise questions, and discern what is best for them as well. They are unable to understand "blind faith"; they are willing to take the leap but want to be able to have at least a little light shone on their way.

Today, we have to use the language and context of our youth and the streets in which too many of them find themselves. We, as a church, have to learn of their culture, however difficult that may be, in order to invite them into a new or renewed life with Christ, a Christ in whom they can see themselves reflected. Images of a blue-eyed, brown- or blond-haired, ethereal, effeminate savior simply alienate them. Black youths, especially our young males, turn to other religions, especially Islam, which they believe are "blacker" (a further evidence of a lack of historical education) and which provide them with much needed self-esteem, discipline, and encouragement.

They can see nothing that they share in the image of Jesus I mention above. But a Jesus as Homeboy, difficult as that may sound, a Jesus who hangs in the "hood," 24/7, dealing with the life-threatening issues and concerns that confront them daily, will speak to them. As liturgist Anscar Chapungo has stated: "The church must reincarnate itself in every culture, as Jesus was incarnated in the Jewish culture."[18]

Over the centuries, Jesus has been transformed from a Jewish peasant to a Renaissance aristocrat to an Anglo or Irish American. It is only in the last decade or so that a Jesus who is Black, Latino, or Asian, a man of the poor and the marginalized, has reappeared, shedding the rich jewels and ornate robes, the manicured nails and styled hair, and the pale white skin of the Jesus of earlier centuries. If the church is to speak to these young people, it must speak their language and become involved in their lives, and this must be reflected in the church's words, its art, its music, and its actions.

But the church must also be willing to listen to our young people and to learn from them They know what is going on in their lives. Just saying "no" to drugs, sex, or any and all of the things that tempt them is a simplistic response because it pays no heed to the actual stark reality of their lives. The church has indeed failed them not only because it does not seem to have rational and realistic answers but also because it does not even seem to know the right questions to ask. At a time when elementary school children are planning their funerals rather than their futures, we must learn how to hear what they are saying to us in the boom and crash of their music and their own overly loud and profane voices.

They, like us, seek liberation. They seek a wonder-working God who will break the chains that tie them to lives of futility and despair.

But that God and God's church must come to them, must listen to them, must speak to them in words that they can understand and appreciate. Then perhaps they will be able, with the grace of God, to respond.

Meanwhile, many of our young black males, and a growing number of our young black females, are in prison rather than in college. We must also realize that we are losing as well those who have "succeeded," those with college degrees, a home in the suburbs, nice clothes and cars. They too see little or no connection between themselves and those they have left behind in the decaying cores of our cities. But they also see no connection between themselves and the church today.

The first lack of connection is due to a failure of memory. Too many successful young African Americans have forgotten that they are the first generation that do not have to picket, struggle, and go to court in order to enter the schools and professions once closed to Blacks. They have forgotten that they stand on the shoulders of countless others, a long cloud of witnesses, stretching back to slavery and Africa itself, who fought not just in order to live or survive but, in time, to thrive.

The second lack of connection is a result of our failure to show the relevance of the church to their lives. We have, in many ways, made them feel unwelcome by not providing them with responsible leadership roles, which by virtue of their education and professional achievements should be theirs by right. Schools and administrative staff of every level are still glaringly White in a church whose face is increasingly one of a darker hue. Our young adults do not need the church or so they believe, but we, the church, certainly need them if we are to survive this millennium. They have found other secular uses for their talents and we suffer their loss.

The third factor is the one which, hopefully, will be corrected as a result of the bishops' pastoral letter: the lack of substantive religious education programs which bridge the gap between high school and middle age. People from age eighteen to thirty-five are the ones we are losing. Their faith is still a child's faith; they have not been challenged or required to grow in their faith. And when they are challenged by adverse circumstances, they drop out rather than attempt to deal with the issues now confronting them. Rather than rigorously engaging their faith and turning to the church for guidance and reassurance, they simply abandon it.

How can we speak to those who do not see the church offering them anything of value? We are a church in crisis. Almost every diocese is suffering from a priest shortage and the average age of priests in the United States is over fifty-eight and rising. The number of Black priests and religious is rapidly declining. Because of the upward mobility of their parents, many Black youth have grown up in predominantly White suburbs, attended predominantly White Catholic or other private schools, and worshiped in predominantly White parishes. As a consequence, they encounter few, if any, symbols or icons of their Black culture, except those from hip-hop videos and coarse TV comedies which distort Black culture. Few are being encouraged to enter religious life or the priesthood, too often seen as alienating and increasingly suspect. How do we reach them? How do we help them recognize and acknowledge that God is a God of love, a God of justice, a God of righteousness, a God of liberation, when they have been taught to be ashamed of their blackness, their history, and especially the work of Martin Luther King Jr. and Malcolm X because both were troublemakers, disrupters of the status quo? What hope can we give them?

Our parish schools and Catholic colleges and universities have had a critical role to play, historically. The goal of the Catholic school has been to prepare Catholic leaders for the future, both of church and nation. Our schools were seen not as the preserve of an elite group, but as an embodiment of the belief that every person possesses the undeniable right to become whatever he or she is capable of becoming.

Do we still have that focus in all of our schools or only in certain ones? Are our colleges and universities, as well as our elementary and high schools, becoming elite preserves of higher learning which ignore the skills and talents, hopes and dreams of another population of U.S. Catholics? Many of them are immigrants, as earlier Catholics were, but now they come from Asia, the Caribbean, Central America, and Africa. Others have been a part of the U.S. and the American Catholic Church since their beginnings.

Our parochial schools today must reclaim their former role as a source for conversion and evangelization. Although their numbers in the inner cities and rural areas have diminished, a Catholic presence must be maintained and, if at all possible, expanded. As we know, many non-Catholic parents send their children to Catholic schools. Yet too often in our schools we do not require the students to take religion courses; we do not discuss the history, traditions, or teachings of the Catholic Church; we do not have them attend Mass or prepare them to participate in the sacraments. If we are too ashamed to proclaim our Catholic faith which forms the foundation for the discipline and academic standards these parents are seeking, then we do need to close these schools for they are not serving the purpose for which they were established.

Fear of "stealing" from another church is no longer the issue, if it ever was, for many, if not most, of these young people have no affiliation with any church or other forms of institutionalized religion at all. They are often seeking a faith home, but feel actively discouraged by their teachers. We must teach our faith as if we believe in it and teach them the history of their people, the African people, and their descendants. We must stop abandoning these young people, playing into the stereotypes that once again leave us marginalized, voiceless, and invisible.

This means also that we must speak to them of their particular calling in the church. I have heard so many young Black men and women speak of their desire to enter the seminary or religious life but who have received little or no encouragement not just from their parents but from their priests and teachers as well. And when they do enter, they find they are required to renounce their culture and traditions to become something other than who they are with their own unique gifts stifled, maligned, and rejected.

The Lack of Sensitivity and Cultural and Historical Training

Training in Black history and culture should be required of those working in the Black Catholic community and the church as a whole. Just as Catholic seminarians today are mandated to study Spanish and take immersion courses in Hispanic culture, they must also be mandated to obtain similar knowledge and experiences of the Black culture. At the same time, it must be recognized that Black culture is not a monoculture but has a multiplicity of strands—from Africa itself with recent waves of immigration, from different countries of South and especially Central America like Panama, from the Caribbean nations of Haiti and the Dominican Republic, Cuba, and the Virgin Islands. In addition, there are the free colored in Louisiana, the free Blacks in Boston, the Spanish-speaking Blacks who helped found Los Angeles and St. Augustine in Florida, and the free slaves who founded their own towns in Kansas and Oklahoma.

To be a Black Catholic means to be one whose faith pervades every aspect of their life. It means loving music in all its forms, from Gospel to classical to hip-hop. It means celebrating a "wonder-working" God in joy and contemplation, for these are not seen as mutually contradictory. We are a holistic (both/and) and communitarian (I/We) people. There is no right or wrong way to be Catholic or to be Black as long as we recognize that, in Christ, we are all made one.

Anyone being assigned to a Black or predominantly Black parish and indeed to any parish where persons of African descent are present in large or small numbers, should receive training in Black history and culture. Highly recommended is the Institute of Black Catholic Studies at Xavier University in New Orleans, a program similar to that of the Mexican American Cultural Center in San Antonio.[19] Participation in the inculturation and immersion programs of the National Black Catholic Congress Office should also be required. Courses of study at these institutions should not only be mandated but also financially supported by each and every diocese regardless of the number of Catholics of African descent they may have within their boundaries. When priests from other countries, including India or Africa, are sent to serve in Black parishes, they too must be culturally and historically educated. The sharing of the dark skin does not guarantee understanding or sensitivity. Unfortunately, too often it has been the opposite, leading to unnecessary alienation, bitterness, and further division in the church.

African American seminarians, novices, and candidates for the permanent diaconate should of course study the complete history of the Catholic Church, a history which must incorporate Black history. This Black history should also be studied by their fellow students. No longer should we allow two thousand years of Black history and theology to be rushed through in a weekend. Rather they must be incorporated as an essential part of the core curriculum in theology and church history.

Isolation and Evangelization

This area is also addressed by *Our Hearts Were Burning Within Us*. If we truly seek to be evangelizers, we must also be willing to be evangelized as well as catechized. True evangelization takes place when a "true and radical conversion" of one's entire being takes place. It is manifested not in the spouting of Bible verses for every occasion nor in outward signs of piety but in the radical transformation of our lives as witnesses to the glory of God incarnated in Jesus Christ. It means living a life of service to all, whoever they may be. It means honoring God, yes, but also honoring God's image reflected in the face of each and every person with whom we come in contact. For how can we claim to love God whom we have not seen and yet hate our neighbors with whom we interact on a daily basis? (1 Jn 4:20) We must reach out to each other, share the good news of Jesus Christ with whomever we come into contact in our everyday lives, not just on Sundays.

All that I have said can be seen as situated in the context of an emerging Black Catholic Theology. A Black Catholic Theology, like all theologies, is particular. It emerges from within us, it is of, by, and for us Black Catholics in the United States. It is also contextual, emerging from our historical experience of slavery, colonialism, Jim Crow segregation, second-class citizenship, and the continuing denial of our humanity. It is holistic, seeing no separation between the sacred and the secular.

We who are Black and Catholic have a rich faith history which has survived innumerable obstacles including the denial of our humanity by our fellow Christian and Catholic brothers and sisters. Yet as St. Anselm stated centuries ago, theology is "faith seeking understanding" and we have been on that journey of seeking to understand faith for a long, long time.

Today, we are finally able to set down in writing, to proclaim in lectures and classes, to preach from the pulpit, and to celebrate at the Eucharistic feast our hard-won understanding of who God is for us as Black and Catholic. God has been with us throughout the long struggle for freedom and liberation both in church and society. To God be the glory, for our God–talk, our theologizing, reflects a God who is and has always been on the side of those unjustly treated, wrongly enslaved, inhumanly treated, and relegated to the margins of society. Our understanding of God is of a "wonder-working" God who calls us forth to serve all who hunger and thirst for justice and righteousness, affirming that which is good while honestly critiquing and if necessary rejecting that which is not conducive to our spiritual and physical well-being.

We seek to share our understanding of God with others, not to put them down or to lift ourselves up but to recognize that God as God cannot be restricted to one way of being, one cultural perspective, one way of celebrating, one kind of prayer, music, or spirituality. For God is God, all encompassing, immanent and transcendent, manifested in this world, participating actively in history but also radically beyond this world, drawing us, challenging us, to the possibilities of new life.

It is the Spirit of God which has empowered us as Black Catholics to speak of our faith and to present that faith without shame, recognizing that we are no longer simply recipients of the ministry of others, but are called to be full participants in the life and mission of the church, on both the local and national levels. We now must take ownership of this church in which we have, for so long, lived marginalized and often alienated lives. We are called to express that ownership in all that we say and do, in our workshops, programs, liturgies, parishes, and every part of our lives.

Today we recognize and affirm that to be Black and Catholic is not a contradiction but a proclamation of historical pride, for to be "truly Black and authentically Catholic" means that we, as an African, American, and Catholic people, have indeed come of age and are now acting in accordance with our adulthood. It means that we continue to challenge the all too prevalent understanding of Roman Catholicism as a Western, Eurocentric religion. We are proclaiming by our presence in the church that there is, indeed, plenty good room in our Father's kingdom for a diversity of expressions of the Catholic faith. We are challenging the Catholic Church to acknowledge that recognition and acceptance of the cultures and heritages of the many peoples who make up the church is no longer a luxury, but a necessity. We are challenging the church to affirm faith in not simply a transcendent Christ but a cultural Jesus, who is embodied in a particular time, a particular context, a particular culture.

As the church finally opens itself to the contributions of peoples of every race and ethnicity, it must also expand its understanding and expression of God and Jesus Christ. This correlates with our understanding of the Incarnation of Jesus Christ. If God became incarnate in a Jewish male, taking on all the characteristics and appearances of that humanity, so must the church, expressive of Christ's body, incarnate itself today in the peoples and cultures with whom it comes in contact. This is not optional; it is a duty.

There is plenty good room in God's kingdom. We must only choose our seats and sit down. As African American Catholics, however, we must also ensure not only that we are doing the choosing but that the seats actually fit us because we have participated fully in their construction and placement at the center, not the periphery, of our church.

As Black Catholics, we are full members of the Catholic Communion. We have struggled for a long time but the journey is nearing its end. As we continue towards that end, we take as our mandate the words of the prophet Isaiah: "They who wait upon the Lord shall renew their strength, they shall mount up with wings like eagles, they shall run and not be weary, they shall walk and not faint" (Isaiah 40:31).

Our faith has not faltered and our Spirit has been renewed. We are truly Black and authentically Catholic. As we continue to deepen our own understanding of ourselves, we offer the gift of ourselves to the Roman Catholic Church, acknowledging that there is still much work to be done. Yet, we have come this far by faith and that faith, in time, will lead us home.

NOTES

1. *What We Have Seen and Heard* (Cincinnati, Ohio: St. Anthony Messenger Press, 1984).
2. Since this talk was given, one of the Black bishops, Wilton Gregory of Belleville, Illionois, has been elected president of the USCCB. Also Dr. M. Shawn Copeland has been elected the first Black president of the Catholic Theological Society of America. She will be succeeded by Dr. Roberto Goizueta, a contributor to this book, as the first Hispanic president.
3. See his *Faith in History and Society: Toward a Practical Fundamental Theology* (New York: Crossroad, 1980).
4. See the essay by Kevin Burke in this book, especially his reflections on J. B. Metz's notion of "subversive memory."
5. In this essay, I use "African American Catholic" and "Black Catholic" interchangeably as do many. However, accuracy would require that I speak of African Americans as specifically those persons of African descent whose origins date from the period of slavery in the United States, whether their ancestors were slaves or free. The term "Black Americans" includes not only African Americans but also those persons of African ancestry who are more recent immigrants to the United States after the end of slavery. The Catholic Church in the United States has always been a church with Black Catholics in it. See Diana Hayes, "Preface: Taking Down Our Harps," in *Taking Down Our Harps*, ed. Diana Hayes and Cyprian Davis, OSB (Maryknoll, N.Y.: Orbis Books, 1998), xi–xv.
6. See "Slavery" in *When Rome Speaks: A Guide to Forgotten Papal Statements and How They Have Changed Through the Centuries*, ed. Maureen Fiedler and Linda Rabben (New York: Continuum, 1998), 82–84.
7. "Slavery," 82–84.
8. "The Church and Racism: Towards a More Fraternal Society," *Origins* 18, no. 37 (February 23, 1989): 617.
9. See Janet Dewert, ed., *The State of Black America in 1988* (New York: National Urban League, 1988), 6.
10. Dewert, *The State of Black America*.
11. Sadly, in light of the contemporary sexual abuse scandal in the U.S. church, too many of those in leadership positions in the church seem incapable of acknowledging their failures and omissions that have had a significantly harmful impact on Catholics of all ages.
12. See the first in-depth history of Black Catholicism in the United States by Cyprian Davis, *The History of Black Catholics in the United States* (New York: Crossroad, 1990).
13. See *What We Have Seen and What We Have Heard*, 8.
14. Cyprian Davis, "Black Spirituality: A Catholic Perspective," in *One Faith, One Lord, One Baptism: The Hopes and Experiences of the Black Community in the*

Archdiocese of New York, vol. 2 (New York: Archdiocese of New York, Office of Pastoral research, 1988), 45.

15. USCCB, *Our Hearts Were Burning Within Us* (Washington, D.C.: USCCB, 1999).

16. See Davis, *The History of Black Catholics in the United States*.

17. See, for example, the July 2001 issue of *U S Catholic* that focuses on the needs and concerns of contemporary American Catholic youth.

18. Anscar Chupungo, *Cultural Adaptation of the Liturgy* (New York: Paulist Press, 1982).

19. Xavier University of Louisiana, a historically Black and Catholic university, was founded in 1915 by the Sisters of the Blessed Sacrament initially as a secondary school. The Institute was founded in 1980 by, among others, Frs. Bede Abrams and Joseph Nearon and Sr. Thea Bowman, OFM.

4

REFLECTING ON AMERICA AS A SINGLE ENTITY: CATHOLICISM AND U.S. LATINOS

Roberto S. Goizueta

At the beginning of his Apostolic Exhortation *Ecclesia in America*, Pope John Paul II challenges us to "reflect on America as a single entity."[1] The use of the singular is appropriate, he suggests, as "an attempt to express not only the unity which in some way already exists, but also to point to that closer bond which the peoples of the continent seek and which the Church wishes to foster as part of her own mission, as she works to promote the communion of all in the Lord."[2] As someone who has always found it rather puzzling that the United States, but one country in North America, could so innocently refer to itself as, simply, "America," I consider the pope's assertion much more than semantic quibbling; in itself, his inclusive use of the singular "America" represents both an acknowledgment of historical reality and, on the basis of such historical honesty, a call to conversion.[3] Indeed, as Cuban American theologian Justo González has observed: "What preposterous conceit allows the inhabitants of a single country to take for themselves the name of an entire hemisphere? What does this say about that country's view of those other nations who share the hemisphere with it?"[4]

HISPANIC/LATINO AMERICAN CATHOLICISM

Pope John Paul II's challenge is today more appropriate than ever, given the recently released U.S. Census Bureau projections indicating that by the end of this century Latinos will constitute one-third of the U.S. population. In the Mexican War, the United States conquered and annexed almost one-half of the territory of Mexico; today we are witnessing the reconquest of that territory, not by the force of arms but by the sweat of the brow, by the very power of the "American dream."

The ongoing Latin American "reconquest" of the United States has even more significance for the Catholic Church in this country. Approximately three-fourths of all Hispanics are Roman Catholic. In ten years, a majority of all Catholics in the United States will be Spanish-speaking. In other words, Catholicism in the United States is *already* an "American" Catholicism whose face, whether we like it or not, is dramatically different from that of the "American Catholicism" so often portrayed in our textbooks, media, sociological studies, or theological research. In *Ecclesia in America*, Pope John Paul II challenges us to acknowledge this reality and to consciously embrace it as a source of renewal for the Church in America.

At the same time, we should remember that what we call the "U.S. Latino" or "U.S. Hispanic" community is, in reality, numerous different communities with different histories. The largest numerically, the Mexican American community actually predates the contemporary United States. Mexicans first became Mexican *Americans* not when they emigrated to the United States but when, in 1848, the United States annexed half of what was then Mexico. Thus, Mexicans did not cross the border; the border crossed them.

The second largest group, Puerto Ricans, have their own unique history, one that also involves conquest. As a result of the Treaty of Paris, which ended the Spanish American War in 1898, Spain ceded the island to the United States, and Puerto Rico eventually became a commonwealth of the United States. Puerto Ricans are thus U.S. citizens, but without representation in the U.S. Congress. The same treaty gave the United States increased influence over the government and economy of Cuba, though Cuba remained technically independent. While Cubans emigrated to the United States throughout the twentieth century, the largest influx occurred after Fidel Castro took power in 1959. Cuban Americans are the third largest Latino group. While all three groups can be found throughout the United States, Mexican Americans are primarily concentrated in the Southwest and Midwest, Puerto Ricans in the Northeast, and Cuban Americans in Florida.

Despite the differences, however, common threads run throughout the histories of the various U.S. Latino communities. All Latinos share, for instance, the historical heritage and experience of "mestizaje" (racial-cultural mixture). The Latin American culture and people are the products of five centuries of racial and cultural intermixing. In North America, the British colonists exterminated the indigenous people; to the South, the Spanish killed millions of Amerindians, either through the illnesses brought from Europe or through outright violence, but the Spanish also intermingled with the native peoples.

In the Caribbean region, the mixture was less between Spanish and Indian than between the Spanish colonists and the Africans brought to the islands as slaves. The result of this history has been a culture that still reflects the influence not only of Spanish culture but also of African and/or Amerindian cultures. And, of course, as Latinos settle in the United States, a "second mestizaje" takes place: immigrants assimilate influences from the larger U.S. culture. So a Mexican *American* is similar but also quite different from a Mexican living in Mexico. Indeed, *U.S.* Latinos are often derided not only by other Americans but also by Latin Americans still living in their native countries, many of whom look down on U.S. Latinos as not quite Latin American. Thus, living as part of a mestizo people means always living on the border, culturally and psychologically; one never feels completely at home on either side.

This same mestizo heritage is reflected in the religious faith of Latinos. At the very heart of the Mexican experience of mestizaje, for example, stands the figure of Our Lady of Guadalupe. The historical experience of mestizaje originated in the violence of the conquest, in the violation of indigenous women by Spanish conquistadores. As the child of violence, the child of the violent European conqueror and the violated indigenous woman, the mestizo/a has historically suffered scorn and humiliation, which he/she has internalized in the form of self-deprecation and self-hatred. In his classic work *El Laberinto de la Soledad*, the great Mexican poet and writer Octavio Paz poignantly described this process whereby the dehumanization suffered at the hands of European conquerors becomes, over generations, a deep-seated self-hatred. The child of the conquistador father and the violated mother is ultimately ashamed of both parents who gave him or her birth through this primordial act of violence.[5]

OUR LADY OF GUADALUPE

However, the appearance of Our Lady of Guadalupe in December 1531 signals a turning point, or axial point in the history of Latin American mestizaje. In the Guadalupe event, "*la Virgen morena*" ("the dark-skinned virgin") appears to an indigenous man, Juan Diego, on a hill outside what is now Mexico City. The narrative recounts several encounters between *"la Morenita"* and Juan Diego, in the course of which she repeatedly assures him that, despite his own sense of worthlessness vis-à-vis the Spaniards, he is her most beloved, favored child. As she continues to reassure him, Juan Diego gradually develops a sense of his own dignity as a child of God. In their first encounter, she commanded Juan Diego to ask the Spanish bishop in Mexico City to build a church on the hill where she had appeared. Juan Diego resisted, arguing that he was not worthy to be charged with such a mission. The Lady insisted, so Juan Diego eventually went to the bishop's palace to make the request. At first, the bishop would not even receive the poor indigenous man. Later, the bishop received but did not believe him. Finally, the Lady gave Juan Diego a "sign" to take with him, a bouquet of flowers she had ordered him to pick from a nearby hilltop. Since all knew that such flowers could not grow at that time of the year, they would recognize the miraculous nature of the sign. So Juan Diego put the flowers in his *tilma*, or cloak. When the indigenous man arrived at the bishop's palace and opened the cloak to reveal the flowers, another miraculous sign appeared, an image of the Virgin imprinted on the cloak. Stirred and convinced by these signs, the bishop relented and ordered that the Lady's wish be granted.

The traditional roles are thereby reversed: the dark-skinned Lady and the indigenous man themselves become the messengers of God, evangelizers to the Spanish Catholic bishop, who is portrayed as the one in need of conversion. In addition, the narrative and accompanying images also exemplify a fascinating religious, symbolic *mestizaje*. Tepeyac, the hill on which the Virgin appeared, was well known to the Nahuas (the indigenous people to whom Juan Diego belonged) as the place where they worshiped the mother goddess Tonantzín. Likewise, the Virgin's clothing was adorned with a mixture of Christian and Nahua symbols.[6]

According to the Mexican American theologian Virgilio Elizondo, the Mexican nation as we now know it could not have emerged if not for the Guadalupe event. In 1531, the indigenous peoples of Mexico had been destroyed by the conquering Spaniards; those who had survived the onslaught were demoralized and in despair. It was at this very moment of deepest anguish that Our Lady of Guadalupe appeared, to accompany them in their suffering, confirm them in their dignity as children of God, and herald the dawn of a new era of hope. Indeed, the image of Guadalupe that Juan Diego saw and the image that, to this day, remains emblazoned on the cloak as it appears in the Basilica of Our Lady of

Guadalupe in Mexico City is that of a pregnant woman (unique in the history of Marian apparitions): La Morenita gives birth to a new people, a mestizo people. Moreover, dark-skinned Guadalupe's ability to relate the Christian faith to the indigenous worldview, adopting and adapting indigenous symbols to the Christian worldview, made possible the evangelization of Mexico.[7]

Though paradigmatic, Our Lady of Guadalupe is hardly the only example of the mestizaje that has taken place not only in race and culture but also in religion. And it is precisely in its religious faith that the U.S. Latino/a community most fundamentally affirms its distinct history and identity as a people of God—and, therefore, a people of dignity—in the face of marginalization and oppression. The popular religion of Latinos/as is that which is most deeply "ours" in a world which consistently attempts to destroy what is "ours," deprecating it as inferior or worthless.[8]

POPULAR RELIGION

The terms "popular religion" and, more specifically, "popular Catholicism" denote much more than a series of religious practices, symbols, narratives, devotions, and so on. Rather, the terms refer to a particular worldview, an epistemological framework that infuses and defines every aspect of the community's life. Popular religion is not only a particular way of being "religious"; it is also a particular way of living life. Indeed, the very distinction between "religion" and life is itself called into question by a faith that is at the heart of every aspect of the community's life. Arguably, then, even that minority of Latinos and Latinas who do not consider themselves explicitly religious reflect—even if only implicitly or obscurely—the worldview, values, epistemological perspectives underlying Latino popular religion and, more specifically, Latino popular Catholicism. For popular Catholicism lies at the very origins, the very heart of the mestizo Latino/a culture itself. "The Spanish-American Roman Catholic Church," observes the Cuban Methodist theologian Justo González, "is part of the common background of all Hispanics—if not personally, then at least in our ancestry."[9]

That heritage is rooted in the history of the Americas. The Christianity that was first brought to the Americas from Europe was a pre-Reformation Iberian, medieval Christianity. In this form of Christianity, religious faith was expressed and lived out primarily through images, symbols, rituals, and religious practices; these were what defined Christian identity. Though the Protestant and Catholic Reformations took place in Europe in the sixteenth century, these did not begin to impact the life of Latin American Christianity until generations later. As European Christians became increasingly concerned with drawing clear lines between what was Roman Catholic (or "orthodox") and what was Protestant (or "heretical"), post-Reformation Christianity attached increased importance to doctrines and confessional beliefs as criteria of "orthodox" Christian faith. In Roman Catholicism, this emphasis on correct doctrine reached an apex in the Council of Trent. Yet Latin America did not experience the full impact of this evolution of Christianity from a faith primarily identified with religious practices, devotions, pilgrimages, symbols, narratives, and the like, to a Tridentine faith primarily identified with dogma.[10]

The Iberian Christianity brought by the Spanish to Latin America "was medieval and pre-Tridentine, and it was implanted in the Americas approximately two generations before Trent's opening session."[11] Theologian Orlando Espín notes that: "While this faith was defined by traditional creedal beliefs as passed down through the Church's magisterium, those beliefs were expressed primarily in and through symbol and rite, through devotions and liturgical practices. . . . The teaching of the gospel did not usually occur through the spoken, magisterial word, but through the symbolic, 'performative' word."[12] As yet, in their everyday lives, Christians did not clearly distinguish creedal traditions from liturgical and devotional traditions; both were assumed to be integral dimensions of *the* Tradition. Espín observes that "until 1546 *traditio* included, without much reflective distinction *at the everyday level*, both the contents of Scripture and the dogmatic declarations of the councils of antiquity, as well as devotional practices (that often had a more ancient history than, for example, Chalcedon's Christological definitions)."[13] The clear distinction between dogma, that is, the *content* of tradition, and worship, that is, the *form* in which that tradition was embodied in everyday life, did not become crystallized until the Council of Trent. "On this side of the Atlantic," argues Espín, "the Church was at least in its second generation, and it took approximately another century for Trent's theology and decrees to appear and become operative in our ecclesiastical scene."[14]

Moreover, the ritual-based Christianity that had taken hold in Latin America had found reinforcement, first, through the analogously ritual- and symbol-based religions of the Amerindians (these similarities thereby facilitating the process of religious *mestizaje*) and, second, through the Baroque Catholicism that would be brought to the "New World" by the Iberian colonizers of the seventeenth century. This latter exhibited a profound dramatic sense of life and the cosmos, as reflected in the many *autos sacramentales* of the period. Such a sense of life-as-theatre and the cosmos-as-stage reinforced the essentially *performative* character of Latin American Christianity, which had been inherited from both the original Iberian missionaries and the indigenous religions.[15]

These popular religious practices reflect and express a particular worldview, one in which the human person sees him/herself as part of a relational network and a temporal continuum embracing all of reality, material, and spiritual. This organic, holistic worldview underlying U.S. Latino culture is at odds with post-Enlightenment notions of time and space, the material and the spiritual, and the person's place within time and space, within the material and the spiritual dimensions of reality.

First, the worldview underlying these popular religious celebrations reflects a particular notion of the human person, a particular "theological anthropology." Indeed, this aspect is often what Euro-Americans find most striking about U.S. Latino popular Catholicism, namely, its decidedly communal character. Whether vis-à-vis one's family, one's barrio, one's ancestors, or God, the Latino/a always exists in relationship. This is evident in the familial character of the Dia de los Muertos celebrations, where so much care is taken to affirm and reinforce family ties, with both the living and the dead. It is also evident in the public, communal processions of Good Friday, where the people accompany Jesus Christ in his Passion, and accompany each other on the Way of the Cross, thereby identifying their own personal struggles with those of Jesus and their companions.

For Latino Catholics, religion and faith are identified with our human relationships; it is in and through these relationships that we celebrate the gift of life. Our relationships are the source of and reason for our celebration, the miracle for which we give thanks. A privatized religious faith is no more conceivable than is an isolated, autonomous individual; these are not reasons for celebration but for mourning.

This individualism permeates our churches and liturgies. The Latino reaction to this individualism is poignantly illustrated in an anecdote recounted by Virgilio Elizondo. He tells of an elderly Mexican woman who, upon seeing the architectural renovations made in her church, became dejected. To make the church more liturgically "correct" all the statues had been removed, save a lone crucifix behind the altar. Asked why she had become so sad when she entered the renovated church, the elderly woman responded, "I know that Jesus is the most important one in the church, but that doesn't mean he has to be alone."

Even Jesus is not an autonomous, self-sufficient individual; even he is defined by his relationships—especially his relationship to his mother, Mary. The special place of Mary in Latino popular Catholicism should thus come as no surprise; if each person's identity is constituted by the relationships and communities which have birthed and nurtured him or her, then it is impossible to truly know Jesus without also knowing his family, especially his mother.

It is important to note that what is taking place in these celebrations is precisely an "identification," an affirmation of identity. In other words, the community here is not merely external to the individual participant, an optional—even if desirable—supplement to the individual's own identity; rather, the community forms and shapes the person's own identity. Here, personal identity is not so much "achieved" through an individual's choices and decisions as it is "received" from one's family, one's community, and, above all, from God.

For Latinos/as, a community is not a collection of fundamentally autonomous individuals who have freely chosen to enter into an association with other individuals ("a voluntary association of like-minded individuals"). Rather, community is the very source of personal identity. Individuals are not the building blocks of community; community is, instead, the foundation of individual personhood. Communion *precedes* personal existence, not the reverse.

This inherently communal theological anthropology is at the heart of the Latino understanding of "identity." The significance of the ritual performance associated with popular religious celebrations is that, like all drama, it forges an identification between the actors, or participants, and their roles, whether these be the roles of the crowds, Roman soldiers, Mary, or Jesus Christ himself in the *Via Crucis*, or the roles of spirits and skeletons in the *Dia de los Muertos* celebrations. It is the very identity between community and self that makes these celebrations so powerful and, conversely, provokes such visceral reactions from Latinos/as when the celebrations are not honored or, as too often still happens in the United States, when the celebrations are discouraged or, in some cases, prohibited. What is at stake in these rituals is the very identity, that is, the very existence of the Latino people as a people—an identity and existence that depend upon the people's ability to maintain an intimate connection with each other, their ancestors, and the divine. Without that connection, the individual Latino/a literally does not exist; to "be" at all is to be-in-relation. Thus, to sever the relationship and, therefore, the means whereby that relationship is forged and affirmed, is to kill the person.

This assertion suggests a second important way in which Latino popular Catholicism reflects an organic worldview, namely, the Latino understanding of the interconnectedness of the material and spiritual dimensions of reality. One of the most widely recognized cultural manifestations of this particular characteristic of Latino culture is the so-called spiritual realism of so much Latino and Latin American literature, where the historical and spiritual worlds often intermingle almost willy-nilly. Events and characters that to an outsider may appear as "magical" or "fantastic" are to the Latino/a merely one more aspect of everyday existence, one more dimension of reality, a reality rich and diverse enough to encompass the "magical" as well as the mundane, the ethereal as well as the material.

Thus, for example, the ritual of placing a deceased relative's favorite foods or photographs on his or her grave, or on a home altar, during the *Día de los Muertos* celebrations in order to give pleasure to the deceased person presupposes a worldview in which there is no clear separation between the spiritual and material realms. Here, the deceased person is *really* present and participating in every aspect of our everyday lives. Indeed, what is called into question by such rituals is precisely any definition of "the Real" which clearly circumscribes the Real, excluding from the definition any non-empirical reality. The non-empirical world is as "real," if not more real than the empirical world—without, however, denying the importance of the latter. This is particularly true of all interpersonal relationships, as these are mediated by love, which can be known as "real" only by experiencing it, not—like empirical reality—by simply "taking a good look." One must certainly evaluate empirically the fruits of love to determine whether it is genuine love, but the empirical results alone are not sufficient: the same empirical action (e.g., giving money to the poor) may be undertaken as an act of genuine love or as an act of egotism, to display one's superiority. The empirical evidence is essential, but not sufficient evidence to determine that love is real.

This intermingling of the spiritual, or transcendent, and the material is also evident in the dramatic re-enactment of the *Via Crucis* on Good Friday, where the line between the Real and the "merely" imagined also becomes blurred. Is "Jesus Christ" really crucified every year at the end of the community's procession? For the many "actors" and participants in the annual *Via Crucis*, one would be hard pressed to deny the reality of the events. The pain, anguish, and tears on the faces of the participants at every *Via Crucis* celebration is evidence that, at least for them, what is transpiring in their midst is indeed real. Time and again, participants describe the experience as events that are indeed "really" happening: the Roman soldier cringes as he pounds the nails through Jesus' hands and feet, or members of "the crowd" find themselves crying real tears as they watch the soldiers whipping Jesus and nailing him to the cross.

A typical Latino mass envelopes the participant in a cacophony of sounds, images, colors, and scents. Whenever possible, the persons with whom one worships are not just looked at out of the corner of one's eye, but are given a heartfelt embrace; the statue of Mary or the crucifix are not just looked at prayerfully, but are touched, kissed, caressed, and embraced. To be in relationship with another is to be in physical contact with him or her, whether that person is a neighbor or Jesus.

This communal, sacramental worldview shared by Latinos and Latinas is becoming increasingly threatened by a U.S. Catholic Church that is often perceived as individualistic, cold, and, therefore, alienating. The Latino experience of worship as a common celebration, involving and affirming the bonds of family and community, too often finds little sustenance in the U.S. Church. It should then come as no surprise that Latinos and Latinas are increasingly attracted to Protestant Evangelical and Pentecostal groups which emphasize these bonds in their worship services, their communal life, and their welcoming outreach to new immigrants. Consequently, these Protestant communities are, in some ways, more familiar to Latino Catholics than is the Catholicism they encounter in most U.S. parishes.

THE PASTORAL CHALLENGE

Understanding and appreciating the significance and richness of Hispanic popular Catholicism are essential if Catholic lay and clerical leaders in the United States are to respond effectively to the Hispanic presence in the Church. (Indeed, it seems almost patronizing to speak of a Hispanic "presence" when, in fact, the church in this country is on the verge of becoming predominantly Hispanic.) It is in and through these rituals, prayers, processions, devotions, and celebrations that Latinos live

their Catholic faith. Whether in the *Posadas*, the Christmastime reenact-
ment of Joseph and Mary's search for lodging, or the *mañanitas* sung to
Our Lady of Guadalupe on the morning of her feast day, or the *Via Crucis* of Good Friday, or the annual pilgrimage to the holy chapel at Chi-
mayo, New Mexico, or the celebrations on the *Day of the Dead*, or the
family prayers offered on the home altar, it is in the daily rhythm of life
in family, neighborhood, and community that Latinos experience the
palpable, loving presence of a God who walks with us.

Consequently, it is important to understand that the *"manera de ser,"*
or "way of being," that I am here calling "popular Catholicism" is, above
all, a way of living centered on *relationship* and, even more specifically, on
family—though by family, I don't mean "nuclear" family but that extended family that, if extended far enough, ultimately unites us to the
larger human, indeed cosmic community. The Catholicism of Latinos,
therefore, tends to be a Catholicism rooted first, not in the parish but in
the home, in the neighborhood.

This fact exacerbates the "invisibility" of Latino Catholics in the
U.S. Church. For Euro-American Catholics are accustomed to gauging
church participation, or church size, by looking out into the pews on
Sunday mornings, or by checking the latest parish registry; the locus of
Catholic identity is the parish. For Latino Catholics, on the other hand,
the locus of identity is not so much the parish as the home.

The reasons for this are many, including important historical reasons. For centuries, Latino Catholics—particularly those who live in
rural areas—have not had access to clergy. Throughout Latin America,
millions of Catholics have no access to a priest except once every month
or two when a circuit-riding priest comes into town to celebrate mass,
hear confessions, perform baptisms, and so on. Moreover, that priest is not
likely to be native-born; even today, the vast majority of Catholic priests in
Latin America are foreign-born. And this in a continent that contains half
of all the world's Catholics. So, if the home is the center of worship for
Latin American and Latino Catholics, this is to a great extent out of necessity; if the faith was going to be nurtured, it would have to be nurtured
by the people themselves. So popular Catholicism is truly "popular," that
is, truly "of the people" in that its roots are not clerical but fundamentally
lay. The ministers who look after the day-to-day spiritual well-being of the
community are not the priests but the *abuelitas*, the grandmothers.

The problem is exacerbated when Latin Americans emigrate to the
United States. Unlike the earlier Irish, Italian, German, and other European Catholics who emigrated to the United States accompanied by

their own clergy, Latinos continue to suffer from a severe shortage of Spanish-speaking clergy. Add to this the fact, mentioned in the earlier part of my chapter, that Latinos tend to experience the typical U.S. Catholic parish as extremely cold and impersonal, and we have the makings of a major ecclesial crisis. Indeed, thousands of Latinos are not waiting around but are seeking out those faith communities where they do experience warm hospitality, vibrant worship, and a church leadership chosen from within the Latino community itself, namely, in Evangelical and, especially, Pentecostal churches. In other words, the attraction of Evangelical and Pentecostal churches is that, in many ways, the "*manera de ser*," or "way of living" Latinos encounter there is more similar to the world of popular Catholicism, with its emphasis on relationships and physical, affective expressions of faith, than is the life of most Catholic parishes.

The challenge is thus a profound one. Given the demographics, the future of Catholicism in the United States is directly dependent upon the future of Latinos in the U.S. Catholic Church. In turn, if Latinos are to remain active in the Catholic Church, a fundamental renewal in church life will be required. We must develop a renewed appreciation of popular forms of worship and develop creative ways of integrating popular religion with the "official" sacramental life of the church, so that each can benefit from the other. We must be able to link together the parish church and the domestic church more effectively. This, in turn, suggests that the Catholic parish community begin to do what so many Evangelical and Pentecostal churches do so effectively, namely, reach out to the Latino community by knocking on doors and establishing person-to-person relationships with the members of that community. In the long run, such a person-to-person approach is the only one that will work in a community that defines itself through its relationships. Such door-to-door ministry is much more important than establishing a hundred diocesan offices for Hispanic ministry, as necessary as these might be.

As the Church comes to define itself more broadly, embracing the world outside the parish structures and the "official" liturgical life of the parish, it will also need to broaden its understanding of pastoral leadership to include the whole range of lay leaders that one finds in the neighborhoods and homes—and most of those leaders are women.

In sum, what is called for is nothing less than a genuine commitment to become what Pope John Paul II has called us to be, a truly *American* Catholic Church, a Church that recognizes, affirms, and witnesses to a Christ revealed on the border, a Christ who transforms that border from a barrier that excludes into the privileged place of God's self-revelation, recognizing among those persons who approach us from "the other side of the border" the messengers of the Good News. Let us not once again, like that Spanish bishop five centuries ago, turn away Juan Diego as he approaches us bearing in his tilma the precious gift of God's great love for *all* of us.

NOTES

1. John Paul II, *Ecclesia in America, no.* 5.
2. John Paul II, *Ecclesia in America, no.* 5.
3. On the notion of "honesty about reality," see Jon Sobrino, *Spirituality of Liberation* (Maryknoll, N.Y.: Orbis Books, 1988).
4. Justo González, *Mañana: Christian Theology from a Hispanic Perspective* (Nashville, Tenn.: Abingdon Press, 1990), 37.
5. Octavio Paz, *El Laberinto de la Soledad* (México: Fondo de Cultura Económica, 1994).
6. For accounts and interpretations of the Guadalupana narrative, see especially the following works: Cloromiro L. Siller-Acuña, "Anotaciones y comentarios al *Nican Mopohua*," *Estudios Indígenas* 8, no. 2 (1981): 217–74; Siller-Acuña, *Flor y canto del Tepeyac: Historia de las apariciones de Santa María de Guadalupe, texto y comentario* (Xalapa, Veracruz, México: Servir, 1981); Siller-Acuña, *Para comprender el mensaje de María de Guadalupe* (Buenos Aires: Editorial Guadalupe, 1989); Jacques Lafaye, *Quetzalcóatl and Guadalupe: The Formation of Mexican National Consciousness, 1531–1813* (Chicago: University of Chicago Press, 1976); Virgilio Elizondo, *Guadalupe: Mother of the New Creation* (Maryknoll, N.Y.: Orbis Books, 1997); Richard Nebel, *Santa María Tonantzin: Virgen de Guadalupe* (Mexico City: Fondo de Cultura Económica, 1995); Stafford Poole, *Our Lady of Guadalupe: The Origins and Sources of a Mexican National Symbol, 1531–1797* (Tucson: University of Arizona Press, 1995); Jeanette Rodríguez, *Our Lady of Guadalupe: Faith and Empowerment among Mexican American Women* (Austin: University of Texas Press, 1994).
7. See Elizondo, *Guadalupe: Mother of the New Creation*, ix–xx.
8. Sixto J. García and Orlando Espín, "'Lilies of the Field': A Hispanic Theology of Providence and Human Responsibility," *Proceedings of the Catholic Theological Society of America* 44 (1989): 75. Among Latino/a theologians, Espín has written most extensively on the notion of popular religion and its role in U.S. Latino culture. Representative works by Espín on this topic include: *The Faith of the People: Theological Reflections on Popular Catholicism* (Maryknoll, N.Y.: Orbis Books, 1992); "Trinitarian Monotheism and the Birth of Popular Catholicism: The Case of Sixteenth Century Mexico," *Missiology* 20, no. 2

(April 1992): 177–204; "Popular Religion as an Epistemology (of Suffering)," *Journal of Hispanic/Latino Theology* 2, no. 2 (November 1994): 55–78.

9. González, *Mañana*, 55.

10. See Espín, *The Faith of the People*.

11. Espín, *The Faith of the People*, 117.

12. Espín, *The Faith of the People*, 119.

13. Espín, "Pentecostalism and Popular Catholicism: The Poor and *Traditio*," *The Journal of Hispanic/Latino Theology* 3, no. 2 (November 1995): 19.

14. Espín, "Pentecostalism and Popular Catholicism," 19.

15. For a description of the profoundly liturgical or aesthetic character of Spanish Baroque Catholicism, see Thomas O'Meara, *Theology of Ministry* (New York: Paulist Press, 1999): 115–16.

5

DEVOTION TO OUR LADY OF GUADALUPE AMONG MEXICAN AMERICANS

Jeanette Rodriguez

E very Roman Catholic girl of my generation most probably grew up with some picture of Mary in her home. Our devotion to Mary was expressed by displaying a picture, a statue, a holy card of her, or the rosary in the home. She is known by many names: Our Lady of Fatima, Our Lady of Lourdes, Nuestra Señora de Cobra, Our Lady of Guadalupe, and so on. These names and others of Mary have captured the mind, heart, and religious imagination of Christians for centuries.

In this chapter I will reflect upon the image of Mary that is mediated through the culture of Mexican Americans. I first became aware of Our Lady of Guadalupe back in the early 1980s when I was involved with farm workers in Salinas, California. As one with roots in Latin America, I had grown up with *La Madre Dolorosa* or the Sorrowful Mother. I was deeply moved by the devotion of Latin American Catholics toward this particular Mary. There was between Latin American Catholics and the Sorrowful Mother an affective bond that supported the people in their daily struggles moving them toward transcendent faith, eschatological hope, and all-inclusive love.

Given my interest in both theology and psychology, I have been drawn to the dynamics of the devotion to Our Lady of Guadalupe at the psychosocial and religious levels, and to the way this devotion is expressed in Christian worship. It has taken scholars over four hundred years to uncover the massive amount of symbolism of Our Lady of Guadalupe and the theological significance of her apparition. This should come as no surprise since the narrative of Guadalupe's apparition is a complex "event" weaving together the symbolism of her image or icon and the chronicle of her deepening relationship with Juan Diego, with the Nahuatl people, and with all who call upon her, love her, and trust in her. Before I present the narrative, perhaps a discussion of the theoretical framework for understanding this Marian devotion might be helpful.

THEORETICAL FRAMEWORK

In my early work on Our Lady of Guadalupe and her role for Mexican American women, I made use of a psychosocial and religious perspective.[1] This perspective includes popular religion and adopts a holistic understanding of the human person as a psychosocial reality. I draw on the works of Jerome Frank, in particular his notion of the "assumptive world," and of William James, especially his understanding of the religious. Frank explains the "assumptive world" as follows:

> In order to be able to function, everyone must impose an order and regularity on the welter of experiences impinging upon him. To do this, he develops out of his personal experiences a set of assumptions. . . . The totality of each person's assumptions may be conveniently termed his "assumptive world." This is a short hand expression for a highly structured, complex, interacting set of values, expectations, and images of oneself and others, which guide and in turn are guided by a person's perceptions and behavior and which are closely related to his emotional states and his feelings of well-being. The more enduring assumptions become organized into attitudes with cognitive, affective, and behavioral components.[2]

The "assumptive world" then includes one's intrapsychic life as well as one's interpersonal relations. It encompasses assumptions formed by perceptions, behaviors, environments, behavioral states, values, expectations, and the way a person images self and others. This assumptive world is also influenced by experience, historical events, choices, and social conditioning that make up a person's psychosocial milieu.

Not all assumptive worlds are the same. Rather, as Frank notes, they vary as experiences and self-images change. How we see ourselves and the world around us, the values we attach to what we see, and our resulting behaviors, all join to form the psychosocial dimension of a person. Recognizing this dimension is vital to the understanding of persons.

Culture plays an important role in this assumptive world. In this chapter, we will understand culture as "socially transmitted, often symbolic, information that shapes human behavior and regulates human society so that people can successfully maintain themselves and reproduce. Culture has mental, behavioral, and material aspects; it is patterned and provides a model for proper behavior."[3] Therefore, to appreciate another person, one must appreciate the person's assumptive world or psychosocial reality and culture. More specifically, to understand the effect of any religious experience on a person, it is necessary to understand how this experience is perceived and valued, and how it motivates behavior—in other words, how it fits into the person's assumptive world and psychosocial reality.

Furthermore, for indigenous communities, psychosocial history is not only individual but communal. A memory like Our Lady of Guadalupe is carried by a people in their historical, social, and political world. This memory of Guadalupe passes on the values contained in one's self-image and includes appreciation of one's own language, culture, and tradition. The image and message of Guadalupe, therefore, are vehicles for cultural memory. As cultural memory, Guadalupe evokes an affectivity that bonds individuals not only to Mary but to each other, thus becoming a key element in the formation of the community, "*un pueblo.*" This preserving, transmitting, and reinterpreting the cultural memory or experience is both an intellectual and an affective process.

To speak of "experience" is to refer to "*la realidad*"—reality. Reality is a synthesis of experiences, which are part and parcel of the totality of a person in a given moment. It entails a psychosocial history that has an impact on the person, whether the individual is conscious of it or not.

What then makes up the experience of Mexican Americans? Words that come to mind are "conquest," "resistance," "borderlands," "born and/or raised in the USA." Another set of accompanying words are "integrity," "anger," "pain," "economically and politically marginalized," and "multiple identities." One may speak of multiple identities in terms of diversity of roles, or in terms of negotiation of multiple worldviews. A description of what it is like to cross between cultures is poetically expressed by the novelist Gloria Anzaldua in her book *Borderlands*:

> Indigenous like corn, the mestiza is a product of crossbreeding, designed for preservation under a variety of conditions. Like an ear of corn—a female seed-bearing organ—the mestiza is tenacious, tightly wrapped in the husks of her culture. Like kernel she clings to the cob; with thick stalks and strong brace roots, she holds tight to the earth—she will survive the crossroads.[4]

This constant crossing is a common thing in Mexican Americans' lives. As they cross back and forth between their dual, sometimes multi-identities, they sometimes feel terribly unaccepted—orphaned. Some do not identify with the Anglo-American cultural values; others do not identify with the Mexican American cultural values. Mexican Americans are a synthesis of these two cultures with varying degrees of acculturation, and with that synthesis comes conflict. One woman told me how she feels: "Sometimes the Latina in me doesn't understand or is in contradiction with the Anglo side of me. Sometimes I feel like one cancels out the other. And I feel like nothing."

Mexican American feminists affirm that they are "more than nothing" and call themselves by the name of the group they most strongly identify with: *mestiza* when affirming both Indian and Spanish heritage, or Chicana when referring to their political Mexican roots. To give another example: because I have roots in Latin America, but was born in the United States, I usually refer to myself as a Latina. But even in this naming, there is no one word that says it all.

To these social and cultural aspects the religious dimension must be added. The term "religion" is used here to refer to an integral part of human experience that enables us to see ourselves in the world in a particular context, namely that of faith, hope, and community. William James defines religion as "whatever it is, is a man's total reaction upon life."[5] This particular definition of religion is helpful because it implies that religion cannot be separated from human emotion and human life. Rather, it is an integral part of human experience.

That religion is not a separate and isolated consideration in human life is best described by James:

> As concrete states of mind, made up of a feeling plus a specific sort of object, religious emotions of course are psychic entities distinguishable from other concrete emotions; but there is no ground for assuming a simple abstract "religious emotion" to exist as a distinct elementary mental affection by itself, present in every religious experience without exception. As there thus seems to be no one elementary religious emotion, but only a common storehouse of emotions upon which religious objects may draw, so there might conceivably also prove to be no one specific and essential kind of religious object, and no one specific and essential kind of religious act.[6]

Joining J. Frank's "assumptive world" with W. James's understanding of religion is critical for understanding the meaning of our Lady of

Guadalupe for Mexican Americans, and this for two reasons. First, Our Lady of Guadalupe is a religious experience. Of course, contemporary Mexican American devotees of Our Lady of Guadalupe do not enjoy a firsthand vision of her, and yet from their faith stories it is undeniable that there is an encounter, a presence, a relationship between them and the Guadalupe that is a vibrant and daily occurrence. Second, even when this is not the case, the Guadalupe's apparition as the primordial experience is kept alive in the cultural and psychological memory of the community. This cultural and psychological memory is concretized in the Guadalupe's picture prominently displayed in many of her devotees' homes. By retelling the story of the Guadalupe's apparition and by their devotion, Mexican Americans share in the memory of the primordial experience. Some internalize this memory so that it becomes for them a personal religious experience, and to the degree in which that memory is faithful, it becomes a primordial experience.

To sum up our discussion of the theoretical framework for understanding the role of Our Lady of Guadalupe for Mexican Americans, the following figures may be helpful. The first figure lists the elements constituting the psychosocial perspective or the assumptive world.

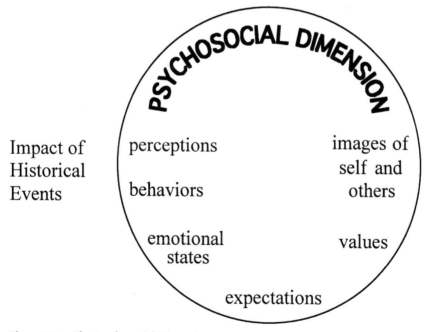

Figure 5.1. The Psychosocial Dimension

In the following two figures, the inner circles show the new components of the psychosocial perspective. The first circle (figure 5.2) shows the religious dimension, which is not a different perspective but is an intrinsic component of the psychosocial perspective. The religious dimension integrates into a person's assumptive world his or her faith, beliefs, and behaviors in relation to the Divine. Given this intrinsic link between the psychosocial and religious, the issues commonly considered as religious must be asked within this broader perspective of human experience.

Within the religious dimension, our focus is on one religious and cultural symbol—Our Lady of Guadalupe—here represented by the third inner circle which includes the story, image, and personal experiences of Our Lady of Guadalupe (figure 5.3).

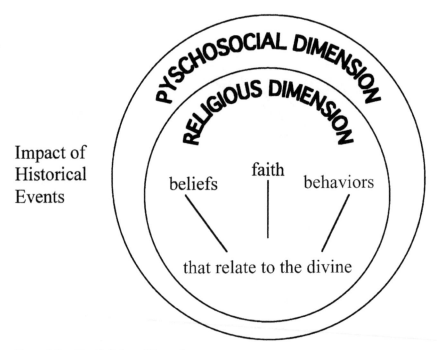

Figure 5.2.   The Religious Dimension

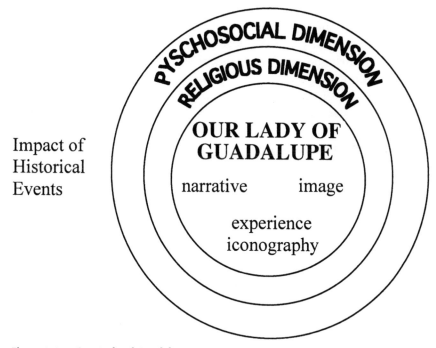

Figure 5.3.   Our Lady of Guadalupe

THE GUADALUPE STORY AS
CULTURAL MEMORY AND STORY OF FAITH

The Guadalupe event is rooted in history. It has a specific content. In my early work on the Guadalupe, I identified her as a cultural memory. This cultural memory is contained in the image of the Guadalupe itself; it is recorded in the Nahuatl document entitled *Nican mopohua* ["Here is it told"]. Like all memories, the cultural memory is a living and dynamic reality. The memory of the Guadalupe is recorded and transmitted in the story of her which her devotees narrate, in their devotional practices in her honor, in the naming of their children after her, and in their celebrations of her feast. Their remembering and evoking of the Guadalupe are mainly a matter of feelings and aspirations, of searching for hope and strength, of maintaining an intimate relationship with her.

Briefly, what is this story of faith and this memory that is transmitted from generation to generation of Mexican Americans? The year is 1531. The *Nican Mopohua* recounts this story and situates it ten years after the Spanish conquest of the indigenous peoples of the Americas. This document is the Nahuatl narrative published in 1649 by Luis Lasso de la Vega, the chaplain at Guadalupe from 1646 to 1656. The title *Nican Mopohua* is taken from the first phrase of the document (variously translated as "Here it is told" or "In good order and careful arrangement").

The protagonist of the story is a fifty-two-year-old indigenous Christian named Juan Diego.[7] The story takes place on Saturday morning, December 9, 1531. Juan Diego is on his way to catechetical instruction. On the way, he passes over the hill of Tepeyac, the ancient site of the great earth goddess Tonanzin. This word, however, is not a name, but a title in Nahuatl meaning "our mother." As he passes over this mount, Juan Diego hears beautiful music. Following this music, he encounters a woman who speaks to him not in the language of the conquistadors but in that of his people, Nahuatl. She says to him: "Juan Diego, the smallest of my children, where are you going?" He must have recognized something about her, because he is reported to fall on his knees and says to her: "I'm going to *your* house to hear the divine things our priests tell us." Tonanzin-Guadalupe answers: "Know and understand, you, the smallest of my children, that I am the holy Virgin Mary, the mother of the true God, *por quien se vive* [for whom one lives]. I have a great desire that there be built here a *casita* [a small house] so that I may show forth my love, my compassion, my help, and my defense, to you, to all of you, to all the inhabitants of this land, to all who call upon me, trust me, and love me. I will heal your pains, your sorrows, and your lamentations, and I will respond to your call."

During this conversation time as it were stopped, and Juan Diego experienced the intimate and consoling presence of the Tonanzin-Guadalupe. Then Tonanzin-Guadalupe said to Juan Diego: "In order for this to happen, you must go to the bishop and tell him that it is I, the Mother of the True God, who speak."

Juan Diego goes to see the bishop, who listens to him kindly, but, as Juan Diego says: "He did not believe me." Later, when Juan Diego meets Tonanzin-Guadalupe again, he suggests that she send someone of greater social standing, so that the bishop might believe, because "I am a nothing, a nobody, a pile of old sticks. You have sent me to places where I do not belong." Tonanzin-Guadalupe replies to Juan Diego that indeed she has many messengers, but it is imperative that *he* be the one to take this message. She sends Juan Diego once again to the bishop and this time with a sign. The sign she gives him consists of different kinds of roses that grow on the desert hill of Tepeyac. Juan Diego returns to the bishop and recounts all that he has seen and heard. Then Juan Diego drops his *tilma* containing the various flowers, and as they fall to the ground, the image of Tonanzin-Guadalupe appears on the *tilma*. It is this image that hangs in the basilica of Mexico City today.

THE STORY IN CONTEXT

The Guadalupe story appears to be a simple one, but one of the things that I have learned from the Mexican American people and in particular from the Benedictine Sisters in Mexico who have a deep devotion to Our Lady of Guadalupe is that it is a story contained within a much larger story. That is, while the story of Guadalupe is a story of faith, it is important to understand the historical reality and context in which it arises. To facilitate the understanding of Guadalupe, those who promote her story and image usually begin with the time before the arrival of the Spaniards to Mexico.[8]

The account of the Guadalupe story regularly begins with Mexico's popular religious history. It highlights the fact that the Mexican people are descendants of the pre-Colombian Olmecs who founded the first important civilization in Mexico around 1200 B.C.E. Because of their abiding influence on the other cultures of the region, the Olmecs are considered the mother of the Meso-American cultures. Through commerce and religion, the Olmecs exercised a deep influence on the cultures of the Toltecs, the Teotihuacans, the Mayas, the Aztecs, Zapotecans, just to name a few. Toward the end of the twelfth and the beginning of the thirteenth century C.E., seven Nahuatl tribes came to the valley of Mexico, one of which was the Aztecs. The Aztecs came from the northwest of Mexico, the land that is known as the mythic Aztlan. The people came under the leadership of their priest, Tenoch. According to the legend, the gods told the priest that the people would see a sign indicating that they had reached the "Promised Land." The sign was an eagle perched on a nopal cactus with a serpent in its beak. This sign was reportedly found in the middle of seven lakes, and as is well known, Mexico City is built upon these lakes.

During the reign of Montezuma I, the Aztec empire was consolidated and its borders were expanded so that by 1502 C.E., when

Montezuma II was chosen emperor, the frontiers of the empire went as far north as Sinaloa in present-day Mexico and as far south as Nicaragua, spanning from east to west, from the Atlantic to the Pacific coast.

What we find in the telling and retelling of the story of Guadalupe is a reclaiming of the greatness of the past, a past whose inception and definition was initiated by the divine. The Aztecs prospered in commerce, arts, and architecture. They built immense temples on the principal island of Tenochtitlan. In this island alone there were seventy-two temples. About 80,000 people inhabited the two islands, Tenochtitlan and Tlteolco, which were joined together by several solid land causeways and two aqueducts. On Tlteolco, the smaller of the two islands, stood Tlatelolco, a great cultural and commercial center, which after the Spanish conquest would become a center for evangelization and learning.

In addition to their exquisite music, song, art, and architecture, the Aztecs also had a highly developed religion. They worshiped Quetzalcoatl (the Lord), along with Ipalnemohuani (a god known as both Father and Mother); Tonatiuh (the new sun); and Ometeotl (the Lord and Lady who are near and close to us). These names, which frequently appear in Nahuatl literature, express God's relationship not only with human beings but also with the cosmos.

This history, which precedes the conquest, serves as the context for the event of Guadalupe's apparition which occurred in 1531, ten years after the conquest. By transmitting the story of our Lady of Guadalupe the narrators intend to remind the people of their glorious ancestry.

All this glorious history was wiped out when Hernán Cortés conquered the Aztecs and asked the king of Spain to send Franciscans to evangelize what they called the New Spain. The Franciscans arrived in 1521 and began their work of evangelization, but this was done in a climate of violent oppression against the indigenous people. To the indigenous people the conquest was a sign that their gods had been overthrown or had abandoned them. Nothing was left for them but to die. This is the context in which the story of Guadalupe emerges. In the midst of death and destruction a great sign of hope and liberation appears—Guadalupe, the mother of the awaited fifth sun, the new Quetzacoatl. Holy Mary of Guadalupe, the maternal face of God, the beloved mother of God, comes to console a suffering people.

The cultural memory of the Our Lady of Guadalupe event endures because it fills a basic need for identity, salvation, hope, and resistance to annihilation. The Guadalupe restores to the Aztecs their human dignity by speaking their once silenced language. She restores not only a lost language but also a way of perceiving the divine. The Guadalupe story retrieves lost symbols and transforms them for a new time. Ultimately, it speaks and continues to speak of a shared experience of a people—a people that suffers. The Guadalupe event and its communal memory recall who Mexicans are as a people, how they were oppressed, and how God sides with them and calls them to liberation and healing. More generally, the Guadalupe event reminds all the oppressed and marginalized people that God takes a stand with and for them and shows them love, compassion, help, and defense.

Through the cultural memory of Our Lady of Guadalupe her devotees recall the promises of compassion, help, and defense that she once made. They experience these promises as a covenant of hope, a hope transmitted through cultural memory and expressed by various means, such as retelling the story, celebrating the feast, visiting the basilica, praying before her image, or working for justice. As a result of Guadalupe's promises, the devotees are committed to preserving her memory by retelling the event of her apparition and by walking humbly and acting justly.

Though mediated through a particular culture (in this case the Mexican and Mexican American culture) the Guadalupe story has a universal significance. It reveals God's presence active everywhere in the world. It is a story about betrayal and trust, destruction and hope, death and resurrection. In many ways it contains the Pascal mystery of the Mexican people and their resurrection into a new creation through the mediation of Tonanzin (Guadalupe).

GUADALUPE IN CHRISTIAN DEVOTION

The Guadalupe story is transmitted through a variety of means: music, songs, flowers, processions, and the like. In particular, the many popular Guadalupe songs clearly convey the key points of the story and the sense of intimacy and trust on the part of the Guadalupan devotees. Two representative samples will be examined here: *Desde el Cielo Una Hermosa Manana* and *Mananitas a la Virgen de Guadalupe*. The first song is sung at every Guadalupan devotion. The second song expresses the people's love and praise for Mother Mary.

Desde El Cielo Una Hermosa Mañana

Desde el cielo una Hermosa mañana
Desde el cielo una Hermosa mañana
La Guadalupana, La Guadalupana
La Guadalupana bajó al Tepeyac.

Su llegada llenó de alegría
Su llegada llenó de alegría
De luz y armonía, de luz y armonía,
De luz y armonía todo el Anahuac.

Por el monte pasaba Juan Diego
Por el monte pasaba Juan Diego
Y acercose luego, y acercose luego,
Y acercose luego al oir cantar.

Juan Dieguito la Virgen le dijo,
Juan Dieguito la Virgen le dijo,
Este cerro elijo, este cerro elijo,
Este cerro elijo para hacer mi altar.

Suplicante juntaba las manos
Suplicante juntaba las manos
Eran Mexicanos, eran Mexicanos
Eran Mexicanos su porte y su paz.

Y en la tilma entre rosas pintada
Y en la tilma entre rosas pintada
Su imagen amada, su imagen amada,
Su imagen amada se dignó dejar.

Desde entonces para el Mexicano
Desde entonces para el Mexicano,
Ser Guadalupano, ser Guadalupano,
Ser Guadalupano es algo esencial.

Madrecita de los Mexicanos
Madrecita de los Mexicanos,
Que estás en el cielo, que estás en el cielo
Que estás en el cielo, ruega a Dios por nos.

Verse one recounts the time and place of the encounter between
Guadalupe and Juan Diego. It was dawn, and the morning was beautiful! Verse two describes how Guadalupe's arrival fills the people with joy,
light, and harmony. All this is said in the language they are familiar with,

and on a site that is sacred to them. Verses three and four describe Juan Diego's journey and his response to the music he hears. The Virgin tells him that it is on this hill that she has chosen to have her altar built. Everything about her was Mexican, even the way in which she held her supplicant hands (verse five). Flowers were painted on her *tilma*, and her beloved image was imprinted upon it (verse six). The last two verses explain why every Mexican is a Guadalupano/a, and to be Guadalupano/a is essential to being Mexican. The song ends in a prayer: "Mother of the Mexicans, you are in heaven, pray for us."

Mañanitas a la Virgen de Guadalupe

Oh Virgen la más Hermosa
Del valle del Anahuac
Tus hijos muy de mañana
Te vienen a saludar

Coro:
Despierta, Madre despierta
Mira que ya amaneció
Mira este ramo de flores
Que para ti traigo yo

Madre de los mexicanos
dijiste venías a ser
pues ya que ves, Morenita
Si te sabemos querer.

Coro: *Despierta. . . .*

Recibe Madre querida
nuestra felicitación
por ser hoy el día grande
de tu tierna aparición

Coro: *Despierta. . . .*

Ricibe Madre querida
nuestra felicitación,
miranos aqui postrados
Y danos tu bendición.

Coro: *Despierta. . . .*

This song is also a very popular song. While dedicated to Guadalupe, it is also used today as a birthday song. In it, speaking in the first person, the people greet the beautiful Virgin of the Valley of Anahuac, and tell her that her children have come to greet her. The chorus asks Guadalupe to awaken, to look at the dawn, and receive the flowers that they have brought her. They avow their love for her, and congratulate her on this great day of her apparition. The song ends with the devotees once again congratulating her and prostrating themselves for her blessings.

OUR LADY OF GUADALUPE

The image of Our Lady of Guadalupe is filled with signs and wonders, an icon leading to a profound understanding of who God is, who we are, and how the world is. In the official account of *Nican Mopohua* Guadalupe introduces herself as the Mother of the God of Truth, the Mother of the Giver of Life, the Mother of the Creator, the Mother of the One Who Makes the Sun and the Earth, the Mother of the One Who is Near. These titles coincide with those given to the Aztec gods and were well known by the Nahuatl people. They identify Guadalupe as one of the Nahuatl people. Indeed, the woman who speaks in their native tongue touches their deepest beliefs and longings.

Moreover, Guadalupe satisfies the desires of the human heart: the desire to be seen, heard, understood, accepted, embraced, and loved. She is the one who defends the marginalized and the poor. She identifies herself as Mother of the True God, the God for whom, through whom, and with whom humans live. As her name indicates, Guadalupe is connected with the supreme creative power who is ever present in human history. She is the symbol of a new creation and a new people. To encounter Tonanzin-Guadalupe is to be assured of God's unconditional love and of one's place in history.

Guadalupe also represents the maternal face of God. This maternal face of God is made visible by the key words Guadalupe uses. She appears to demonstrate her love, compassion, help, and defense; she hears and heals all of the people's miseries and suffering. She does not appear or convey her message to the center of power and domination, but to the poor and the abandoned. As the God of Abraham and of Sarah once did, she stands with the vanquished "in the spirit of the feminine." In this experience, the marginalized have a special relationship with God, one that is especially meaningful for those who do not enjoy any power in this world. This relationship with Our Lady of Guadalupe—and thus with God—is a means of empowerment. The devotee is not made subordinate to her but rather is invited into a relationship of mutuality and reciprocity.

As well, Guadalupe's apparition affirms the marginalized culture of the Nahuatl people. She makes herself present in the roses Juan Diego gathers from the hillside. Her presence is ushered in with music which he hears as she approaches. Juan Diego's encounter with Guadalupe in flowers and song enhances the cultural symbols of the Nahuatl people, as flower and song—*flor y canto*—together manifest the presence of the divine. The Nahuatl people make use of botanical elements to express truth and beauty. The beauty and fragrance of flowers can only come forth from a healthy root, and since God is the root of truth and beauty, flowers are God's manifestation to the world. As signs of God's presence, they make human thought rise toward God, providing us with the opportunity to enter communion with God in mind and body.

NOTES

1. See my *Our Lady of Guadalupe: Faith and Empowerment among Mexican-American Women* (Austin: University of Texas Press, 1994).

2. Jerome Frank, *Persuasion and Healing: A Comparative Study of Psychotherapy* (New York: Schocken Books, 1961), 27.

3. John Bodley, *Cultural Anthropology: Tribes, States, and the Global System* (Mountain View, Calif.: Mayfield Publishing Co., 2000).

4. Gloria Anzaldua, *Borderlands—La Frontera: The New Mestiza* (San Francisco: Aunt Lute Books, 1987), 78.

5. William James, *The Varieties of Religious Experience* (New York: New American Library of World Literature, 1958), 51.

6. James, *The Varieties of Religious Experience*, 40.

7. For a full account of the apparition of Guadalupe, see my *Our Lady of Guadalupe*, 31–36.

8. For a fuller presentation of this historical context, see my *Our Lady of Guadalupe*, 1–15.

6

"PRESENCE AND PROMINENCE IN THE LORD'S HOUSE": ASIANS AND PACIFIC PEOPLE IN THE AMERICAN CATHOLIC CHURCH

Peter C. Phan

The title of this chapter is borrowed from the United States Conference of Catholic Bishops' December 2001 statement on Asians and Pacific people in the American Catholic Church. With this statement the bishops intend "to recognize and affirm with loving assurance their [Asians and Pacific people] presence and prominence in the Lord's house." They also hope that this pastoral statement "will facilitate a fuller appreciation of their communities in our local churches and will encourage Asian and Pacific Catholics to take on active leadership roles in every level of church life."[1] Of the "presence" of Asians and Pacific people in the American Catholic Church today there is little doubt; nor is there any gainsaying that their number is growing by leaps and bounds. Whether they also enjoy "prominence" in the church is, however, a matter for debate. For the moment, their "prominence in the Lord's house" is arguably more a pious desideratum than a descriptive statement.

This chapter intends to explore ways to transform the "presence" of Asian and Pacific Catholics into "prominence" in the American Catholic Church. At the outset, however, one thing must be made absolutely clear. The purpose of this quest for a "fuller appreciation" of Asian and Pacific Catholics on the part of the American Catholic Church and for their "active leadership roles in every level of church life" must not be a jockeying for more clout and influence either by dislodging Anglo Catholics from their positions of power in the church or by competing with other ethnic groups such as the Latino/as, the Blacks, or the Native Americans for a larger piece of the ecclesiastical pie. That would a shameful betrayal of the Christian vocation to humble and generous service in the spirit of Jesus who came not to be served but to serve (Matthew 20:28). Rather, the goal is to enable these newcomers to live out their Christian calling fully and vigorously in their new adopted church and country while preserving and renewing their diverse cultural, spiritual, and religious traditions, without which they would not be able to bring a distinctive contribution to the church and the society that are now their home.

WHO ARE ASIAN AND PACIFIC AMERICAN CATHOLICS?

Thanks to the 1965 Immigration Act which abolished the quota system which had systematically favored immigrants from Western Europe and severely limited the number of immigrants from Asia, Africa, and the Middle East, and because of war and economic distress, in the last forty years a large number of refugees and immigrants have come to the United States from Latin America and the Caribbean, the Middle East, Africa, Eastern Europe, and last but not least, from Asia and the Pacific Islands. The U.S. Census Bureau defines Asians and Pacific Islanders as "any of the original peoples of the far east, Southeast Asia, the Indian Subcontinent, or the Pacific Islands." Census 2000 counted 11,898,828 Asians in racial categories that include East, South, and Southeast Asians and mixed-raced Asians, a whopping 50 percent increase since the previous decade.[2] The Asian and Pacific American population is expected to double by 2010.

American Asians and Pacific People

By now, for most Americans, especially those living in large metropolises of the East and West coasts, Asian and Pacific people have become a familiar sight. In some cities the black-haired and brown-skinned Asians and Pacific people, together with their Latino/a look-alikes, have outnumbered the Anglos! But even those who live in rural areas and in middle America cannot fail seeing Asian faces as anchors in evening newscasts and morning talk shows and as commentators and comedians on television (of course, with flawless English and unaccented enunciation!). Occasionally the media report on the activities of Asian and Pacific governors, members of the Senate and the House of Representatives, and cabinet members. In many communities certain services such as laundry and nail care are provided predominantly by Asians who are praised for their manual dexterity, courtesy, and industriousness.

Asian and Pacific students have long enjoyed the reputation of being whizzes at math, engineering, and computer science. But by no means are they bookish nerds. There are Asian U.S. Olympic athletes and national sports champions, noted for their grace and nimbleness on ice as well as for their brute force in such muscular sports as football and basketball. More than their fellow Americans, college students tend to have Asian and Pacific friends with whom they enjoy sharing Mongolian barbecue beef, Chinese wonton and sweet and sour pork, Vietnamese *pho* and spring rolls, Indian tandoori chicken, Japanese sashimi and sushi, Filipino *escabeche*, Korean *kim chee*, and Thai *som tum* in ubiquitous Asian restaurants. Marriages between Asians and Pacific Islanders on the one hand and Anglos or Blacks or Latino/as on the other are still few and far between, but the number is on the rise and the report, admittedly anecdotal, is that they are by and large successes, especially when the wife is Asian or Pacific.

In addition to enriching the American culture, cuisine, and ethnic composition, Asians and Pacific Islanders also bring to the United States, besides their brands of Christianity, their non-Christian religious beliefs and practices, and it is a rare American city that is not dotted here and there by Buddhist pagodas, Zen meditation centers, Confucian and Taoist shrines, Hindu temples, Muslim mosques, and places of worship of lesser-known religious sects and movements.

By now one thing is abundantly clear: Asians and Pacific people are here to stay, and their number is increasing dramatically. But far from being homogeneous, they are characterized by a dizzying diversity and myriad differences in languages, ethnicity and race, social classes and political ideologies, educational levels and professional skills, cultures and religions, and anything else imaginable. Hence, the obvious question: Who are Asians and Pacific people? The simplest answer is that Asians are people who hail from Asia and Pacific people from the Pacific Islands in the South Pacific Ocean. It may be argued, however, that as umbrella terms "Asian" and "Pacific" are almost meaningless since they stand for so much variety and diversity. Asia refers to East Asia, Southeast Asia, South Asia, Central Asia, and Near East (or Middle East) and is composed of fifty-three countries and territories. As for Pacific states there are no less than twenty-six.[3]

To speak first of Asia, everything in this continent today tends to fascinate and frustrate the visitor with its sheer size and dizzying variety.[4] Asia is the earth's largest continent and is home to nearly two-thirds of the world's population, with China and India accounting for almost half of the total population of the globe. Economically, the Asian continent is characterized by extremes, with some countries such as Japan, Singapore,

Taiwan, and South Korea having a technology and industry rivaling those of the most advanced countries in the West, while others are suffering from abject and widespread poverty such as Vietnam, Cambodia, Laos, North Korea, Bangladesh, Afghanistan, and several of the countries in Central Asia which have recently regained their independence.

Among the Asian poor, women fare the worst: female illiteracy is much higher than that of males, and female babies are more likely to be aborted than male ones. On the other hand, Asia is often depicted as the land of the mysterious and fabulous East abounding in sensual delights and bodily pleasures of every kind. Leaf through a glossy travel brochure and your fantasy will be transported to exotic and erotic paradises such as those in Thailand, Hong Kong, and Indonesia, where the tourist industry has wrought devastation on the Asian cultural and moral landscape, especially with a brisk business in women and child prostitution.

Politically, Asia displays a confusing array of regimes, from democracy to dictatorship, from separation of church and state to theocracy and state religion, from laissez-faire capitalism to orthodox communism. Culturally, the variety is no less breathtaking. An intricate mosaic of vastly different languages, races, ethnic groups, and cultures, Asia is far more heterogeneous than any other continent of the world. For example, in terms of languages, India has, beside Hindi as the official language, hundreds of other languages; China, in addition to Mandarin, has more than one hundred different spoken languages; the Philippines has eight major languages and eighty-seven dialects. The official language of Indonesia is Bahasa Indonesia, but there are hundreds of other languages used by different ethnic groups such as the Balinese, Batak, Dayak, and Madurese.

Most significantly, Asia is the cradle of the world's major religions, including Christianity, Hinduism, Judaism, and Islam. Asia is also the birthplace of many other religious traditions such as Zoroastrianism, Buddhism, Jainism, Sikhism, Confucianism, Taoism, and Shintoism, not to mention the many tribal or indigenous religions with their own beliefs and rituals. All of these religions and religious traditions have not disappeared, as Christian missionaries have predicted. On the contrary, many of them have recently experienced a vigorous revival and even have begun missions to the West!

As for the Pacific people, there are currently 874,414 Pacific Americans. This population includes U.S. citizens from Hawaii, Guam, the Northern Marianas, and American Samoa as well as people from the Federated States of Micronesia, the Marshall Islands, Palau, Tonga, Western Samoa, and others. Pacific people are composed of three indigenous groups: Polynesians, Micronesians, and Melanesians. Linguistically, French and English are commonly used, but there are almost one thousand indigenous languages spoken in the Pacific Islands!

According to Census 2000, of Asian Americans, the largest group consists of the Chinese (92,432,585), followed by Filipinos (1,850,314), Indians (1,678,765), Vietnamese (1,122,528), Koreans (1,076,872), and Japanese (796,700). Smaller Asian ethnic groups include Bangladeshis, Cambodians, Hmongs, Indonesians, Laotians, Malaysians, Pakistanis, Sri Lankans, Taiwanese, and Thais. Among Pacific Islanders, the most numerous group is Hawaiians (140,652), followed by Samoans (91,029), Guamanians (58,240), and Tongans (27,713).[5] More than two-thirds of Asians and Pacific Islanders live in seven states: California, Hawaii, Illinois, Texas, Louisiana, New Jersey, and New York.

Asian and Pacific American Catholics

Despite the fact that Jesus was born in Western Asia and that the history of the church in Asia is as old as Christianity itself, Christians currently make up only a little more than 3 percent of the Asian population, and that after more than five hundred years of Christian missions.[6] Except for the Philippines, East Timor, and the Marianas where some 85 percent of the population are Catholic, only a very small percentage of the population of most other Asian countries are Christian. South Korea and Vietnam are exceptional, with about 8 percent of their population being Catholic.

By contrast, in the United States, Christians form the majority of Asian and Pacific Americans. Most of them are Catholic (with a minority belonging to the Eastern Catholic Churches, in particular the Syro-Malabar and Syro-Malankara Churches, estimated at 500,000) and a sizable number are Protestant, mostly Presbyterian and Baptist. It is estimated that among Asian and Pacific Americans there are 300,000 Chinese Catholics (out of 2,432,585); 1,536,590 Filipino Catholics (out of 1,850,314); 285,390 Indian Catholics (out of 1,768,765); 325,000 Vietnamese Catholics (out of 1,122,528); 74,887 Korean Catholics (out of 1,076,872); 31,887 Japanese Catholics (out of 796,700); 20,290 Samoan Catholics (out of 91,029); 48,921 Guamanian Catholics (out of 58,240); and 4,000 Tongan Catholics (out of 27,713).[7] There are thirty dioceses that have more than 100,000 Asian and Pacific Catholics, notably Los Angeles, Honolulu, Brooklyn, San Jose, Oakland, San Francisco, Orange, Seattle, New York, and Chicago.[8] Asian and Pacific

Catholics make up the third largest of people of color (after the Latino/as and the Black) and account for about 2.6 percent of the Catholic population in the United States.

WHAT DO ASIAN AND PACIFIC
PEOPLE BRING TO THE UNITED STATES?

Because of their ethnic, racial, linguistic, cultural, and religious pronounced differences from other newcomers to the United States, Asian and Pacific refugees and immigrants stand out more conspicuously, compared with, let's say, recent immigrants from Eastern Europe (who blend in well with Anglos), Latin America (who may be mistaken for U.S.-born Mexicans), and Africa (who may be taken to be Blacks). By the same token, their cultural and religious contributions to their adopted country appear more distinctive. Needless to say, the danger of stereotyping is very high when generalizing about the cultural and religious gifts these Asian and Pacific strangers bring to their host country, just as the myth of their successful adaptation to the life in the United States without help from state and federal governments (the "model minority" perception) has been used to paper over the marginalization of a significant segment of the Asian and Pacific population and to denigrate other minority groups in an effort to divide and conquer. With this danger in mind one can read with sympathy the following description of Asians by Pope John Paul II:

> The people of Asia take pride in their religious and cultural values, such as love of silence and contemplation, simplicity, harmony, detachment, non-violence, the spirit of hard work, discipline, frugal living, the thirst for learning and philosophical enquiry. They hold dear the values of respect for life, compassion for all beings, closeness to nature, filial piety towards parents, elders and ancestors, and a highly developed sense of community. In particular, they hold the family to be a vital source of strength, a closely knit community with a powerful sense of solidarity. Asian peoples are known for their spirit of religious tolerance and peaceful co-existence.[9]

It is well known that many Asian and Pacific people, in particular youth and the elderly, are experiencing serious difficulties in maintaining and fostering these traditional values in their new country where premium is placed on individual autonomy and rights and immediate satisfaction of personal needs rather than on obligations to the common good and sacrifice of individual self-fulfillment for the welfare of the family. This emphasis on individual freedom and self-fulfillment threatens in particular the Asian and Pacific family structure with its clearly delineated roles of men and women and its extended family system. Like other American families, Asian and Pacific families have to face increasing problems of divorce, teenage pregnancy, gangs, runaways, drug abuse, and suicide. Youth have to constantly negotiate between two cultural worlds, caught between their parents' wish to educate them in the old values and the pressure of their peers to conform to the new ones. The elderly, unable to communicate even with their grandchildren who often do not speak their mother tongues, and lacking a requisite knowledge of the English language and American culture, suffer from isolation and loneliness.

In spite of these problems and challenges, there is no doubt that Asians and Pacific people bring to the United States distinctive gifts without which American culture and history would be much poorer. Among these many and diverse gifts two may be highlighted as of particular significance, namely, the peculiar experience of being an immigrant and the ideal of harmony.

Being Betwixt and Between

It is a well-known sociological fact that many immigrants and refugees, especially after they have successfully inserted themselves into the mainstream of the society, tend to look down upon the newcomers, even those from their original countries, as social parasites. Saluted as the "model minority," they preach the gospel of total self-reliance and advocate a "color-blind" policy, forgetting the many special benefits of affirmative action that enabled them to arrive to where they are now. They black out the intense struggle and suffering they underwent as refugees and immigrants, perhaps because they were too painful for them.

In this context, the experience of being a refugee and an immigrant needs to be recalled, and memories of physical and emotional suffering retold, for the sake not only of erstwhile refugees and immigrants but also of those born in the United States who run the risk of taking peace and justice and material abundance for granted as their birthright. What is then the existential condition of a transnational immigrant and refugee? From the findings of various social-scientific research, it is clear that its most obvious features include violent uprootedness, economic poverty, anxiety about the future, and the loss of national identity, political freedom, and personal dignity.

In addition to this dehumanizing condition, transnational migrants also exist, from a cultural perspective, in a "betwixt-and-between" situation that is the hallmark of marginalization. They live and move and have their being between two cultures, their own and that of their host country. In this "in-between" predicament they belong to neither culture fully yet participate in both. To be betwixt and between is to be neither here nor there, to be neither this thing nor that.

Spatially, it is to dwell at the periphery or at the boundaries, without a permanent and stable residence. Politically, it means not residing at the centers of power of the two intersecting worlds but occupying the precarious and narrow margins where the two dominant groups, that is, those of the homeland and those of the host country, meet, and consequently being deprived of the opportunities to wield power in matters of public interest. Socially, to be betwixt and between is to be part of a minority, a member of the marginal(ized) group. Culturally, it means not being fully integrated into and accepted by either cultural system, being a *mestizo/a* or *mulato/a*, a person of mixed race. Linguistically, the betwixt-and-between person is bilingual but usually does not achieve mastery of either language and often speaks them with a distinct accent. Psychologically and spiritually, the immigrant does not possess a well-defined and established self-identity, but is constantly challenged to forge a new sense of self out of the resources of the two, often conflicting, cultural and spiritual traditions.[10]

This betwixt-and-between predicament, while a source of much soul-searching and suffering, can be an incentive and resource for a creative re-thinking of both cultural traditions, the native and the foreign. Being in-between is, paradoxically, being *neither* this *nor* that but also being *both* this *and* that. The immigrants belong fully to neither their native culture nor to the host culture. By the same token, however, they also belong to both, though not fully. And because they dwell in the interstices between the two cultures, they are in a position to see more clearly and to appreciate more objectively, both as insiders and outsiders ("emically" and "etically"), the strengths as well as the weaknesses of both cultures, and as a result, are better equipped to contribute to the emergence of a new, enriched culture. Hence, to be in-between as an immigrant is to-be-*neither*-this-*nor*-that, to-be-*both*-this-*and*-that, and to-be-*beyond*-this-and-that.[11] Being an immigrant, while a painful condition, can turn out to be a blessing for both the immigrants themselves and the society of which they are the new members. It offers to immigrants the opportunity to appreciate the riches of their own cultures which they run the risk of taking for granted in their own native countries, just as fish do not realize the vital need of water while swimming in it. On the other hand, it allows the host society to be constantly renewed and enriched by the immigrants' cultural and religious resources.

The Quest for Universal Harmony

In addition to this dynamic of renewal and enrichment which every society needs to perpetuate and revitalize itself, Asians and Pacific people bring to the American society, which is under the constant threat of being torn apart by its multiple polarities, a sense of universal harmony and reconciliation.

There is no doubt that harmony is central to Asian cultures and religions. It is said by the Theological Advisory Committee of the Federation of Asian Bishops' Conferences to constitute "the intellectual and affective, religious and artistic, personal and social soul of both persons and institutions in Asia."[12] After expounding the concept of harmony as espoused by Asian philosophies, primal religions, and religious traditions (including Hinduism, Buddhism, Confucianism, Taoism, Christianity, and Islam), the Theological Advisory Committee concludes: "It is clear there is an Asian approach to reality, an Asian understanding of reality that is profoundly organic, i.e., a world-view wherein the whole, the unity, is the sum-total of the web of relations, and interaction of the various parts with each other."[13]

Thus, harmony is not simply the absence of strife but lies in acceptance of diversity and richness. Nor is it merely a pragmatic strategy for successful living amidst differences. Fundamentally, it is an Asian *spirituality* involving all the four dimensions of human existence: the individual self, and his or her relationships with other human beings, the material universe, and God. This is clear from the teachings of various Asian religious traditions. The Hindu way is marked by a quest for a harmonious integration of the whole and the parts at all levels: individual, social, and cosmic. The cosmos is sustained by a harmonious order; society is held together by the order of *dharma* (law); and the individual achieves harmony by observing the cosmic order and society's moral and religious code.

In Buddhism, harmony in the individual, which leads to liberation from suffering, is achieved by following the so-called Eightfold Path: right speech, action, and livelihood (*sīla* [morality]); right effort, mindfulness, and concentration (*samādhi* [meditation]); and right understanding and thought (*prajñā* [wisdom]). According to Zen Buddhism, harmony in the individual is the unity of body and mind in all the person's activities and produces enlightenment and a deep sense of peace. Because of the unity between body and soul, physical practices such as proper sitting position, regulating the breath, and composing the mind are necessary conduits to spiritual enlightenment.

Harmony in the individual leads to harmony with other human beings, which, according to Confucius, include the family, the nation, and the world. According to the Chinese Sage, one cannot pacify the world without governing one's nation well; one cannot govern one's nation well without ordering one's family rightly; and one cannot order one's family rightly without achieving mastery over oneself. And self-mastery is achieved by living out five relationships correctly: between ruler and subject, between husband and wife, between parent and child, between elder sibling and younger sibling, and between friend and friend. Each of these five relationships implies a set of obligations and duties, and if one fulfills them rightly, one lives in harmony with oneself and with others.

Furthermore, because the human person is a microcosm reflecting the macrocosm, she or he must also be in harmony with nature or the cosmos. This harmony is particularly emphasized in Taoism. Chuang Tzu, the greatest Taoist after Lao Tzu, declares: "The cosmos and I were born together; all things and I are one." In practical terms, cosmic harmony demands that humans maintain a healthy and sustainable ecosystem, avoid the pollution of the environment, reduce the consumption of energy resources, and in general develop an attitude of reverence for, a contemplative posture toward, and a sense of oneness with the Earth and non-human creation.

Finally, harmony in oneself, harmony with one's fellow human beings, and harmony with the cosmos are rooted in and strengthened by harmony with God. This harmony with the Divine is the fundamental teaching of Islam, an Arabic term meaning "surrender." To be in harmony with God, we must in all things submit to God's holy will in mind, heart, and action. We must, to use a Confucian expression, learn to know and fulfill the mandate of Heaven.

The Asian spirituality of harmony will shape human life as an unfolding of right relationships. As the Theological Advisory Commission affirms: "Starting from consciousness of the God-given harmony within oneself, one moves into harmonious relationship with one's fellow humans; then one spreads out to be in harmony with nature and the wider universe. This unfolding and realization of right relationship within oneself, with the neighbors and the cosmos leads to the summit experience of harmony with God."[14] Harmony, says the Theological Advisory Commission, "is neither a compromising with conflictual realities, nor a complacency about the existing order. Harmony demands a transformative attitude and action, to bring about a change in contemporary society. This can be provided only by a prophetic spirituality which exercises charitable but courageous criticism of the situation."[15]

This spirit of complementarity and harmony is strongly insisted upon by the Asian bishops at the Asian Synod when speaking of the Asian cultural and religious values as forming the basis of the Asianness of the church: "All of this indicates an innate spiritual insight and moral wisdom in the Asian soul, and it is the core around which a growing sense of 'being Asian' is built. This 'being Asian' is best discovered and affirmed not in confrontation and opposition, but in the spirit of complementarity and harmony. In this framework of complementarity and harmony, the Church can communicate the Gospel in a way which is faithful to her own Tradition and to the Asian soul."[16]

WHAT DO CATHOLIC ASIANS AND PACIFIC PEOPLE BRING TO THE AMERICAN CATHOLIC CHURCH?

Asians and Pacific people are not only citizens of the United States making contributions to the various aspects of its life but also members of the Body of Christ to whose growth and well-being they must add their share. In fact, their contributions to some areas of church life have been visible and easily quantifiable, such as institutional membership, financial giving, and church constructions. Of significance, too, is their contribution in terms of priestly and religious vocation to both the diocesan clergy and religious orders (this is true particularly of Vietnamese Catholics). In fact, there are currently three Asian American bishops—Chinese, Vietnamese, and Filipino.

In addition, Asian and Pacific Catholics have made other distinctive contributions, less visible but no less important, to the American Church. The following deserve brief mentioning: their witness to the faith through martyrdom, their popular devotions and community activities, their commitment to interreligious dialogue, their solidarity with the poor and the oppressed in their native countries, and their contribution to theology.

Witness in Suffering

Despite their many differences, Asian and Pacific churches share one common characteristic, namely, they all were until recently, and many still are, "mission territories." Their histories are steeped not only in the heroic sacrifices of legions of foreign missionaries but also in the blood of countless martyrs.[17] So far 487 Asian Catholics have been declared saints or blessed: Japan (187), Korea (100), Vietnam (98), China (87), Thailand (8), India (4), Philippines (2), and Sri Lanka (1). There are also several martyrs among Eastern Catholics. Of course, many more Asian Catholics have died for the faith. In Vietnam alone, it is estimated that 130,000 Catholics were killed for the faith during the persecutions from 1625 to 1886.

Asian Catholics' readiness to bear witness to the Christian faith even unto death is a timely reminder that Christian discipleship requires a radical denial of self and a faithful following in the footsteps of Jesus. Such a reminder is all the more necessary for Christians living in a culture obsessed with personal self-fulfillment and the individual's unalienable rights to "life, liberty, and the pursuit of happiness." As Pope John Paul II declares with reference to the efficacy of martyrdom as a means of evangelization: "However important programs of formation and strategies for evangelization may be, in the end *it is martyrdom which reveals to the world the very essence of the Christian message*."[18]

Popular Devotions and Community Activities

The faith life of American Asian and Pacific Catholics is nourished of course by the Word of God and the sacraments. But it is also nurtured by popular devotions. Indeed, the cultivation of popular devotions is a distinguishing characteristic of many Asian and Pacific communities and constitutes one of their important contributions to the American Church. While post–Vatican II Catholics tend to downplay popular devotions for their alleged superstitious character and their tendency to alienate people from this-worldly concerns, Asian and Pacific Catholics have continued to foster practices of popular devotion (e.g., Marian devotions, pilgrimages, novenas, Benediction, prayers to the saints, etc.) and derive much spiritual nourishment from them. Every August, the Marian celebrations organized by the Congregation of Mary Coredemptrix in Carthage, Missouri, draw an astonishing crowd of some 40,000 Vietnamese Catholics. Filipino Catholics are known as "pueblo amante de Maria" and have many popular devotions of their own.

Intimately connected with popular devotions is another major characteristic of Asian and Pacific Catholic communities and parishes, that is, the flourishing of communal activities, often in tandem with sacramental celebrations (especially baptism, marriage, and funerals), certain calendrical feasts (e.g., the New Year), and cultural customs (e.g., death anniversaries). In addition, there are a large number of pious associations (e.g., confraternities, sodalities, youth groups) which provide the laity with the opportunity to exercise leadership and be actively involved with the community, especially in its liturgical and spiritual life. Recently, more modern associations have been added, such as Bible study groups, charismatic prayers group, RENEW, Cursillo, etc. These associations with their manifold activities are reliable indices of the vibrancy of Asian and Pacific American Catholic communities.

Interreligious Dialogue

As has been mentioned earlier, Asia is the birthplace of almost all world religions. Scratch the surface of every Asian Catholic and you will find a Confucian, a Taoist, a Buddhist, a Hindu, a Muslim, or more often than not, an indistinguishable mixture of all of these religions. Asian and Pacific Christians live within a society in which they rub shoulders daily with non-Christians and have direct experiences of the moral values and spiritualities of non-Christian religions. They are socialized into these values and spiritual traditions not only though formal teachings but also, and primarily, through thousands of proverbs, folk sayings, songs, and of course, family rituals and cultural festivals. Many Asian and Pacific Catholics do not find it strange or difficult to inhabit different religious universes. It is this rich and varied religious heritage, latent but pervasive, that Asian and Pacific Catholics bring with them to the United States and will be one of their most significant contributions to the American Church.

Solidarity with Poor and Oppressed People Back Home

Most if not all first-generation Asian and Pacific immigrants experienced socioeconomic deprivation, extreme in some cases, and political oppression before coming to the United States. This experience of poverty and oppression makes Asian and Pacific Catholics highly sensitive to the sufferings and needs of their fellow nationals. This sense of solidarity with victims of poverty and oppression is shown vividly in generous collections of money and materials to support the church as well as their relatives back home, and in their organizations to fight for human rights, especially for religious freedom, in their home countries.

An Asian Theology: Liberation, Inculturation, Interreligious Dialogue

Last but not least, an Asian and Pacific theology is emerging in the United States. Such a theology is built on the three main foci of the church's mission today, namely, liberation, inculturation, and interreligious dialogue.

Asian and Pacific American theology, as implied by its "hyphenated" character, is neither purely Asian/Pacific nor purely American. An offspring of the marriage of two widely divergent cultural and religious heritages, it bears all the marks of a *mestizo*, a mixture of the two traditions. On the one hand, with the United States as its home, it faces questions and challenges proper to its social location, and has at its disposal theological resources different from those of its countries of origin. On the other hand, it cannot but dig deep into its Asian/Pacific religious and cultural traditions to find resources to answer these questions and meet these challenges. Paradoxically, while neither fully Asian/Pacific nor fully American, an Asian and Pacific American theology is *both* Asian/Pacific and American, embodying the resources, methodologies, and characteristics of both theologies, and in this sense, will be richer than either theology, Asian/Pacific or American, by itself. An Asian and Pacific American theology is by nature an *intercultural* theology, forged in the cauldron of the encounter between two vastly different cultures.

As *Asian/Pacific*, this emerging Asian Pacific American theology owes a great debt to the theologies that have been developed in Asia throughout the last two millennia to inculturate the Christian faith. The Saint Thomas Christians of the Syro-Malabar and Syro-Malankara Churches with their Syrian theological heritage; Persian Christians of the Nestorian tradition who came to China during the T'ang dynasty in the seventh and eighth centuries; members of various religious orders, in particular the Jesuits, who evangelized the greater part of Asia in the seventeenth century; legions of missionaries, both Catholic and Protestant, who revived the church's evangelizing enterprise in Asia in the nineteenth century; Asian bishops and theologians of our own times, all of these people have made permanent contributions to the elaboration of Asian theologies.

Among these contributors pride of place must be given to the Federation of the Asian Bishops' Conferences (FABC), founded in 1970, and its various offices and institutes. The sheer quantity, thematic comprehensiveness, and theological depth of the documents they produced in the last thirty years dwarf all the previous theological achievements of the Asian Churches and allow Asian theologians to stand tall in the company of their Western colleagues. In addition to its teachings on various substantive issues, the FABC has advocated a new way of being church and of doing theology in Asia. This new way consists in a triple dialogue, namely, dialogue with Asian cultures (inculturation), with Asian religions (interreligious dialogue), and with Asian peoples, especially the poor (liberation). Asian American theology will have to undertake this triple task of liberation, interreligious dialogue, and inculturation, and in this way will contribute significantly to contemporary theological method and ecclesiology.

As *American*, this aborning American Asian and Pacific theology must be done with a full and vivid awareness that its social location is one of power and domination. For good or for ill, Asian and Pacific Americans are citizens of a country that will remain for the foreseeable future the world's only superpower, military and economic. Rich or poor, they all benefit from the wealth and power of their adopted country. The passport they hold carries much weight around the world and entitles them to the basic human rights denied to citizens of other countries. They participate in an economic system of free market that has been by and large successful in producing financial gains for those able and willing to embrace it.

These political and economic advantages do not, however, accrue to Americans without heavy costs to others. As a group, Americans consume a disproportionate amount of the earth's resources, with deleterious effects on the ecology, to enjoy and maintain their sacrosanct "American way of life." Their political and military leaders do not hesitate to use their country's massive military arsenals to crush not only the so-called axis of evil but also those who are perceived to threaten America's "vital interests" and its citizens' "life, liberty, and the pursuit of happiness." Through globalization, the United States extends its political and economic hegemony throughout the world, exercising new forms of imperialism and colonialism. As a result, the gap separating America from other countries grows larger and the very few rich get richer, while the teeming masses of the poor (among them, women and children in particular) get poorer.

Asian and Pacific Americans, willy-nilly, are part of this system of racial, gender, economic, and political exploitation and domination. None of them now have clean hands, even though they may have come to the United States from poor and oppressed countries. But precisely because of their backgrounds and histories, Asian and Pacific Americans cannot forget or ignore the cries and tears of their fellow citizens in their adopted countries and of the people in their former homelands, when they attempt to do their own theologies. Of necessity, Asian and Pacific American theology must be guided by the concern for the liberation of those who are deprived of the minimal conditions for a decent human life. Its beacon must be God's kingdom of peace and justice and love.

At the conclusion of their statement on Asian and Pacific Catholics in the United States, the American bishops summarize well the contributions of these new members of the American Church:

> By being authentically Christian and truly Asian in the footsteps of Christ, they have brought to us a more profound understanding of what it means to be truly Catholic. They have taught the Church in the United States the meaning of harmony; the necessity of dialogue with their cultures, with other religions, and with the poor; a renewed sense of family loyalty; the unity between diverse cultures and diverse Catholic church communities; and the closeness of all God's creation.[19]

The emerging American Catholic Church, built on the joys and hopes, tears and laughters, sacrifices and celebrations of millions of old and new immigrants, must be the church which invites and welcomes into its loving bosom people of diverse races, ethnicities, sexual orientations, cultures, and religions. It must be the home where people, so diverse in everything yet so unified in faith, hope, and love, can embrace one another in their differences and uniqueness, accept others as other, strengthen and enrich one another with their distinctive gifts, forgive and be reconciled with one another, and in this way reflect in the world the infinite unity in diversity of God.

NOTES

1. United States Conference of Catholic Bishops, *Asian and Pacific Presence: Harmony in Faith* (Washington, D.C.: United States Catholic Conference of

Catholic Bishops, Inc., 2001), 1. Henceforth, *Asian and Pacific Presence.*

2. For helpful histories of Asian Americans, see Ronald Takaki, *Strangers from a Different Shore: A History of Asian Americans* (New York: Penguin Books, 1989); Stanley Karnow and Nancy Yoshihara, *Asian Americans in Transition* (New York: The Asia Society, 1992); and David Palumbo-Liu, *Asian/American: Historical Crossings of a Racial Frontier* (Stanford: Stanford University Press, 1999).

3. For a list of Asian countries and Pacific States and their maps, see *Asian and Pacific Presence*, 36–40.

4. For a brief description of the Asian context, see Pope John Paul II's Apostolic Exhortation *Ecclesia in Asia*, which was promulgated in November 6, 1999, following the Special Assembly for Asia of the Synod of Bishops (April 19–May 14, 1998). For a study of the Asian Synod and the English text of *Ecclesia in Asia*, see Peter C. Phan, ed., *The Asian Synod: Texts and Commentaries* (Maryknoll, N.Y.: Orbis Books, 2000).

5. See *Asian and Pacific Presence*, 6.

6. For current statistics on Christians in Asian countries, see Peter C. Phan, *In Our Tongues: Perspectives from Asia on Mission and Inculturation* (Maryknoll, N.Y.: Orbis Books, 2003), 204, note 11. For a lively and up-to-date account of Asian Christianity, see Tom Fox, *Pentecost in Asia: A New Way of Being Church* (Maryknoll, N.Y.: Orbis Books, 2002). For a brief history of Asian Christianity, see Pope John Paul II's Apostolic Exhortation *Ecclesia in Asia* (November 1999), no. 9. The document is available in Phan, *The Asian Synod*, 286–340.

7. See *Asian and Pacific Presence*, 9.

8. For a complete list of these dioceses, see *Asian and Pacific Presence*, 7.

9. *Ecclesia in Asia*, no. 6.

10. See Peter C. Phan and Jung Young Lee, eds., *Journeys at the Margins: Toward an Autobiographical Theology in American-Asian Perspective* (Collegeville, Minn.: Liturgical Press, 1999), 113. For this understanding of marginality, see Jung Young Lee, *Marginality: The Key to Multicultural Theology* (Minneapolis: Fortress Press, 1995), 29–76. See also Eugene Brody, ed., *Behaviors in New Environments: Adaptation of Migrant Populations* (Beverly Hills, Calif.: Sage Publications, 1979), especially Eugene Brody, "Migration and Adaptation," 13–21 and Henry P. David, "Involuntary International Migration," 73–95.

11. This predicament is not dissimilar to what Fernando Segovia describes in his evocatively titled essay "Two Places and No Where on Which to Stand: Mixture and Otherness in Hispanic American Theology," in *Mestizo Christianity: Theology from the Latino Experience*, ed. Arturo L. Bañuelas (Maryknoll, N.Y.: Orbis Books, 1995), 29–43. From an anthropological point of view, this "in-betweenness" is equivalent to a liminal situation as described by Victor Turner. As such, "in-betweenness" intimates anomaly, insofar as people in liminality are no longer what they were ("neither-this") nor are they yet what they will be ("nor-that"). However, they are not stuck in the present but project themselves

toward the future ("beyond-this-and that"). They live between memory and imagination. On memory and imagination as two inseparable modes of doing theology, see Peter C. Phan, "Betwixt and Between: Doing Theology with Memory and Imagination," in *Journeys at the Margins*, 113–33.

12. The Federation of Asian Bishops' Conferences (FABC) is a voluntary association of episcopal conferences in South, Southeast, East, and Central Asia, established and approved by the Holy See in 1972. Its Plenary Assembly meets every four years in ordinary session. It has a central committee, a standing committee, a central secretariat, and several offices. The documents of the FABC and its offices are available in three volumes: Gaudencio Rosales and C. G. Arévalo, eds., *For All Peoples of Asia: Federation of Asian Bishops' Conferences. Documents from 1970 to 1991* (Quezon City, Philippines: Claretian Publications, 1992); Franz-Josef Eilers, ed., *For All Peoples of Asia: Federation of Asian Bishops' Conferences. Documents from 1992 to 1996* (Quezon City, Philippines: Claretian Publications, 1997); and Eilers, ed., *For All Peoples of Asia: Federation of Asian Bishops' Conferences. Documents from 1997 to 2001* (Quezon City, Philippines, 2002). These documents will be cited as *For All Peoples*, followed by the years of publication in parentheses. The document of the FABC's Theological Advisory Commission is entitled *Asian Christian Perspectives on Harmony* and is found in *For All Peoples* (1992), 229–298. The text quoted is located on p. 276.

13. *For All Peoples* (1992), 276.

14. *For All Peoples* (1992), 286–87.

15. *For All Peoples* (1992), 290.

16. *Ecclesia in Asia*, no. 6. See also the Final Statement of the FABC's Seventh Plenary Assembly in *For All Peoples* (2002), 8–9.

17. See Francis X. Clark, *Asian Saints* (Quezon City, Philippines: Claretian Publications, 2000).

18. *Ecclesia in Asia*, no. 49.

19. *Asian and Pacific Presence*, 31.

7

UNDERSTANDING CHURCH AND THEOLOGY IN THE CARIBBEAN TODAY

Gerald Boodoo

From the time Caribbean theologians attempted to forge a local theology in the late 1960s and early 1970s, three approaches have been taken.[1] The first uses cultural and literary sources as well as analyses of racial and social stratification to understand the complex cultural patterns of the Caribbean. This approach predominates and is most evident in liturgical practices which adopt a wide range of local expressions. An obvious advantage of this approach is that it grounds theology squarely in regional expressions and fosters a more respectful understanding of the local context and the experiences arising from it. The main disadvantage is that the use of social scientific analysis often replaces theological analysis and theology is reduced to sociology. The theologian becomes an informed observer.

The second approach views the struggle for justice in its social, political, and economic dimensions as central to the Christian message. Its advantage is a clear demand for justice and an unequivocal commitment to realize the gospel in our present context as an imperative of the kingdom of God. Theology here takes on a more prophetic role and uses social scientific theory as a basis for understanding existing human relationships. The main disadvantage is that this type of analysis, though appropriate for uncovering the mechanisms of colonization and conquest that have shaped the Caribbean, is not adequate for analyzing the current contexts of post-colonialism and globalization. This approach tends to be anachronistic, more adequate for an earlier period when there were clear-cut distinctions between employer and laborer, oppressor and oppressed, slave owner and slave, foreigner and native. With the blurring of these distinctions, psychologically as well as geographically, an analytical method that can more adequately account for the personal, social, regional, and global complexities of the region is needed.

The third approach uses historical method for theological reflection. Rather than viewing the Caribbean as a theater of dominant personalities or absentee landlords, the region is understood as a space shaped by its material relations. The Caribbean must be looked at over a long period of time to expose interrelating and overlapping cycles of human agency, culture, and economics. The advantage of this approach is that it clearly takes into account the complexity of material relationships in the region and can describe the many levels of its public life. In addition, this approach rehabilitates the traditional non-theological disciplines of philosophy and history. The main disadvantage is that whereas it was clear in times past that history was the stage where one could see the hand of God at work and philosophy could help understand the nature and mind of God, this new historical method is solely about exposing the stark reality of the context. As necessary as this analysis is, it is not yet theology proper and must find a way to make theologically useful the insights gained from the historical analysis or run the risk of reducing theology to a sophisticated anthropology.

These three approaches are not mutually exclusive, and theologians in the Caribbean frequently use aspects of some or all of these approaches for theological reflection. What is apparent is that Caribbean theologians are still searching for appropriate theological methods.

THEOLOGICAL METHOD

This methodological concern is echoed in the published report of the first conference on "Catholic Theology in the Caribbean Today" held in St. Lucia in 1994. One of the essays that explicitly discussed theological method was Michel de Verteuil's entitled "A Theological Method for the Caribbean Today."[2] De Verteuil makes two important preliminary points. First, that the church in the Caribbean "should be a communion, one where poor people experience that they are not poor, but full creative members of the communion," and second, the Caribbean Church "should be a sign and an effective instrument of social transformation."[3] De Verteuil goes on to state that theological method must be adapted to the people of the region. By this he means first that theology must also be done in settings other than traditional theological schools, such as the local parishes; that it must be taught at times convenient to the people; that its language must not be abstract; and that it must come to terms with the fact that in the future the main practitioners of theology will be the laity. Next, de Verteuil proposes *lectio divina* as a theological method adequate for the Caribbean today. This method promotes a community theology that "is a way of reading the Bible by which in reading biblical texts we read our own stories."[4] According to de Verteuil, this method allows practitioners of theology to recognize God's work in their daily lives, their culture, and their ancestors. It is an inculturated way of doing theology that allows an interpretation of what is going on in society, the development of a critical consciousness, and the discovery of a people's dignity as God's people.

De Verteuil's proposal of *lectio divina* as an adequate theological method for the Caribbean today is an interesting one. He clearly wants to make theological reflection, and by implication the church, accessible to, and engaged by, all members of the church. This method "de-elitizes" who does theology and where it is done. Who determines what the church should be will also be decided differently. In breaking down personnel and location barriers this method seeks to empower local communities with a theological voice and as a consequence, to transform the shape of the church.

De Verteuil's proposal appears to go beyond the three approaches mentioned earlier and to offer an effective way to construct a genuinely contextual theology. However, though helpful in fashioning a contextual theology for the Caribbean, *lectio divina* is essentially a "soft" combination of the first two theological approaches. This in no way demeans the method or its practitioners, but places it in a proper perspective. Any theology using this method still has to find an analysis to account for the current complex context of the Caribbean and then interpret this analysis in theological terms. Such analysis will not likely be found by reading of the bible. To the linkage between bible reading and social analysis must be added theological reflection, which in turn relies not on the already made link between bible reading and social analysis but on its own relationship with the theological tradition. Hence, the role of a formally trained theologian remains indispensable; in the end it is the theologian who situates, guides, and directs the theological reflection. Admittedly, all Christians are implicit theologians by virtue of baptism. Nevertheless, the more Christians become explicit theologians through formal theological training, the more powerful is the theological voice in the region. To bring this about is the great value and success of *lectio divina*.

Other presentations were also made at the St. Lucia conference and it will be helpful to review them briefly. Gabriel Malzaire suggests that the region must work toward "a Caribbean Christian Civilization" to help all persons reach their ultimate goal, namely, the knowledge of God.[5] In his view, to promote a Christian civilization, the Caribbean Church must fulfill the following tasks. First, it must be a church of compassion. Second, it must offer healing and welcome to its members. Third, it must engage in dialogue. Fourth, it must be a liberating church, defending each person's dignity, self-respect, and uniqueness. Fifth, it must be a prophetic voice promoting justice for all. Sixth, it must pay special attention to women who are the majority of its membership. Finally, it must educate and equip its members to realize these tasks.

Joseph Harris, then rector of the Regional Seminary of St. John Vianney and the Ugandan Martyrs in Trinidad, suggests ways to move from the model of dominance in ministry and formation for ministry to one of partnership. He argues that the local Christian community should be the locus and agent of ministerial formation.[6] The role of the church is "to reveal to the world the way in which God acts."[7] To do so in the Caribbean, says Harris, the church must exist as a response to God in the structures and forms of the cultures of the Caribbean. It must be an agent of cultural transformation by offering an alternative consciousness to that of the dominant culture. The church must also be a sign of the kingdom of God by transcending all cultures. It must be as well a community committed to the basic equality of all persons, fostering mutuality and co-responsibility in ministry. Consequently, the church must encourage true participation of all its members in various ministries and in decision making. Finally, the church must be missionary, that is, it must not be turned in on itself but must recognize, relate to, and act responsibly toward the world. These tasks require that education for ministry must not be geared toward a mere acquisition of factual knowledge but must be rooted in experience aiming at promoting critical awareness and dialogue with various religious traditions.

My own presentation, "On the Christian Presence in the Caribbean,"[8] attempts to show that theological reflection in the region in the 1990s has not moved beyond that of the 1970s. This lack of progress was because the church in the Caribbean and its theology were too caught up in the dominant ideologies of the 1980s and 1990s. Hence, despite efforts to make the church more local, Caribbean ecclesiology still remains mired in the legacy of colonialism. The way forward seems to require a theological method that is able to expose and break the colonialist ideology and at the same time generates and sustains a space for a new identity and future possibilities for the church. This space, I suggest, is one of both confrontation and belonging.

In his "Attempt at Indo-Inculturation"[9] Martin Sirju broaches the interreligious dimension of the church. Through a comparison between Mary and the Hindu goddess Lakshmi he unveils what he considers to be similar structures between Catholic and Hindu beliefs. He argues that church in the Caribbean must find ways to relate to religions apparently very different from Christianity and must take into account its East Indian population.

In "Keep Traditions, Local Customs, Religion and Christianity Together"[10] Lambert St. Rose claims that "the ecclesiology of the first Christian community was never severed from the anthropology or ontology of the Jewish people. . . . They saw no contradiction or distinction in belonging to the Church and belonging to their respective traditions."[11] St. Rose urges therefore an inculturation of the Caribbean Church by means of the anthropology and ontology of the Caribbean peoples.

Patrick Anthony's "Changing Attitudes Towards African Traditional Religion and the Implications for Afro-Caribbean Tradition in St. Lucia"[12] explores the relationship between faith and culture in the region. Through an examination of the Kélé ceremony, an African Traditional Religion ritual in St. Lucia, Anthony demonstrates "the potentials of Kélé for catechesis on the Eucharist, one of the central tenets of Catholic doctrine."[13] Anthony argues that the Christian faith can be enhanced and not necessarily diminished by local and indigenous religious customs.

In the final presentation, Robert Schreiter, the only international observer invited to the conference, asks and answers the question "Why a Caribbean Theology?"[14] He highlights three distinct contributions the Caribbean can make to theology. First, the complex ways in which the region forges its identity through an encounter of persons, cultures, and religions and the hybrid forms of this identity are instructive for the rest of the world. Second, the Caribbean cultural artifacts such as music, art, and literature are a source of enrichment for others. Third, the Caribbean's history of the encounter among different religious traditions is helpful for interreligious dialogue. Schreiter encourages the elaboration of a theology in the Caribbean "that is true to the kind of Church you hope to be . . . the kind of Church you want to be."[15]

CHALLENGES TO CARIBBEAN
THEOLOGY AND CHURCH

Despite their different themes and approaches, these presentations all share the concern that Caribbean theology be contextual, that is, it must be generated by and reflect the Caribbean context. This contextual theology in turn shapes the Caribbean Church. Being contextual, Caribbean theology need not choose between competing theological methods nor does it need to label itself exclusively as feminist, cultural, revisionist, liberationist, or whatever. It is free to use various methods and theologies. The only question is whether it is genuinely contextual. This of course is where differences of opinion may arise. Whose reading of the context is genuinely representative of it? Here the study of theories of interpretation (hermeneutics) is necessary. How is the context to be read so as to be represented faithfully and accurately? More importantly, how is the context to be understood so that what Church could and should be is understood?

In response to this question, the presentations generally argue that account must be taken of the history and culture of the Caribbean. Thus they reflect the three approaches mentioned earlier and signal continuity with the theological reflection in the region since the late 1960s. But this also implies that the forty-year-old wish for a contextual theology for the Caribbean Church has not yet been fully fulfilled. How then does one go about constructing a contextual theology for the Caribbean today?

There is no doubt that the Caribbean Church is still gripped by the legacy of colonialism. But in a post-colonial and globalized world, aspects of which can readily be found in the Caribbean, colonialism alone cannot account for the stagnation that has taken place. In my judgment, the problem is not lack of will but fear. There is the fear of attempts at forging new interpretations of the history of the Caribbean. There is also the fear of trying to look beyond the uniqueness of the Caribbean culture to the uniqueness of relationships in the Caribbean. In different ways all of the presentations hint at this problem. In particular, Harris and Schreiter have pointed it out most clearly. Harris says that the "great difference between first and third world Christianity is the fact that there is continuity in the spiritual journey of first world peoples, a continuity that is absent in the third world."[16] On his part, Schreiter says "the very complex way that you have been and continue to put together your identity, in terms of encounter, and the way you engage each other. . . . What we are seeing in the world today is that the really strong people, the people who are going to be able to live in increasingly pluralist societies—and all the world is becoming like that—are the people who have mixed and do mix."[17]

The real issue then is not restoring continuity through cultural belonging but understanding how the lack of continuity and homogeneity in Caribbean peoples' religious and spiritual journeys has shaped them and their history. It would seem that the rest of the world is becoming more like what the people of the Caribbean already are. In some strange ways, the rest of the world can be either the future or the past of the Caribbean depending on the choices the region makes. These choices must be guided by an understanding of what people in the region are called to be and to do as church in the Caribbean. The question then becomes: how is the Caribbean person to understand this call?

VOCATIO/CALLING

That the church now exists in the Caribbean does not mean that it will continue to exist or that it should exist simply by virtue of its being there. If there is no contextual understanding of why the church is in the Caribbean and what it is there for, it will be simply an institution concerned solely with its own survival and not with the well-being and flourishing of the local people. In a region such as the Caribbean where there are breaks in the historical, cultural, and religious lives of the people, the notion of church as a reality called for particular purposes is of great importance. It would be helpful therefore to explore briefly the notion of *vocatio* and unfold its implications for the church in the Caribbean region.

Vocatio [calling] has its origins in the Hebrew scriptures. There it basically means "to give a name" or "to name." Giving a name to someone is laying claim to, or taking possession of, or appointing a person for a particular task implied in the name given (Gen 17:5; 32:28). In the Christian scriptures, the term has a more narrow meaning and refers to a people being *called*, or *to be called* for a divine mission and destiny (Rom 8:29 f). In this calling, God takes the initiative and the people's role is to respond to that call. Calling also suggests a separating out, a kind of consecration.

The Christian scriptures uses the word *klesis* (Ephesians 4:1) to mean calling, invitation, vocation, state, or position in life. This call is not just a call; it is a call to follow. In early Christian literature, *klesis* is used almost exclusively in a religious sense. It is almost always a heavenly or divine call, an invitation to enter into the kingdom of God.[18] From *klesis* is derived the word *ekklesia* meaning church or assembly.

Vocatio is therefore a calling that is related to the Christian community, a community of believers. *Vocatio*, in a very real sense, is rooted in the community, and, in light of what is suggested in the Hebrew Scriptures, we may say that the divine call is to the community, the *ekklesia*. Therefore, the context for the discernment and exploration of the vocation is the community engaged in critical reflection. This means that *vocatio* must also be historical in nature and that it cannot be disconnected from the context of a people struggling for meaning within that context.

As faith seeking understanding, theology is the systematic study of the Christian faith. In the contemporary modern, post-colonial, and global context however this can be more concretely understood as critical reflection on historical praxis in the light of faith.[19] This definition emphasizes human action (praxis) as the point of departure for all reflection and as the determining factor in the encounter with the Lord and with other persons. Human actions in history therefore shape theological reflection.

As critical reflection, theology takes a critical position regarding all the issues affecting the Christian community. In this sense, theology is a second step following actions for historical transformation in the church and in the world. Thus understood, theology "fulfills a prophetic function insofar as it interprets historical events with the intention of revealing and proclaiming their profound meaning."[20] Theology therefore combines both wisdom and rational knowledge with a view toward "ecclesial praxis"; in other words, it is the critically reflective action of the concrete community of which one is a committed and active member.

In light of the foregoing reflections, *vocatio* is not just a calling rooted in and related to the Christian community, but is also a call *to* the community. Not only does the community shape the call, the call/calling also shapes the community. So the community and the call/calling are the same vehicle for theological reflection. The community as a whole is called, just as each of its members is called to fulfill the comprehensive calling of the wider community.

This leads to an important ecclesiological insight, namely, the church, as called, is deeper and greater than the institutional church. Indeed, understood most fully as the sacrament of the reign of God, it goes beyond the boundaries of confessional churches. The universal church is no longer understood as communion of denominational churches but as communion of the diverse histories and cultures of humankind in which the church is located. In a sense, it is because of the particularity of local and regional churches with their distinct histories and cultures that the universality of Christianity is possible.

In the Caribbean context, this theological understanding of *vocatio* requires that the church that is called understands its calling as a charge to respond to the needs of the local community and not as a call to promote its institutional well-being and expansion at the expense of the local community. This means that a secure, respected, appreciated, and assertive local community will lead to a secure and vibrant institutional church. Any lack of the integral connection between the local community and the church is a sign that a healthy theology of the role and place of the church in the local community and, conversely, of the role of the local community as church in the universal church is missing.

This theology of *vocatio* serves to challenge the choices that have been made in building the local church in the Caribbean. Fundamentally, it questions who has the power to discern and make decisions and the exercise of that power. What is being asked is how one should understand and use power in the context of the Caribbean Church.

THE POWER THAT IS JESUS CHRIST

At the 2001 annual convention of the Catholic Theological Society of America, in his paper "*Missio Ad Gentes:* An Asian Way of Mission Today"[21] presented in the World Church Theology Group, Leo Kleden spoke of European missionaries going to Asia from positions of political, cultural, and religious superiority. By contrast, today Asian missionaries come to the West from a position of weakness. According to Kleden, "in comparison to the former missionaries from Europe, the Asian missionaries today seem to be sent empty handed. This fact is their weakness and should be their strength as well." I will quote at length from Kleden's unpublished paper:

> First of all, it is their weakness. Many of them come from a rural background with their cultural heritage in the pre-modern worldview. But very soon they enter into the modern world through education and schools. Now they are further confronted with the postmodern condition. They live in tensions between three worldviews

which are not easy to harmonize. These missionaries need much more time than their predecessors not simply to learn another language and culture but also to orient themselves within the tensions and conflicts between those worldviews. And what can they concretely do in their mission? We know that former missionaries preached the Gospel, taught catechism, and baptized people; but they were also actively involved in education, health care, and in promoting social and economic development. All these were considered integral parts of their mission. Today many of these jobs have been taken over by the state or secular institutions. When new missionaries are sent from Asia to Europe or America they cannot get involved in these fields. Even in teaching catechism or preaching many local people can do better than they. From the religious perspective, former missionaries went to the countries where mythic-religious values were still predominant, whereas new missionaries are thrown into secularistic society. It is much more difficult to preach the Gospel in the post-Christian situation. On the other hand, this kind of weakness can and should be the strength of the new missionaries. Here is a golden opportunity to follow the example of the first disciples of Jesus who were sent empty handed but who were inspired by the Spirit of the Crucified and Risen Lord. The empty handed approach is therefore possible if their heart is full of faith, with the willingness to serve others as the Lord Jesus. Through the Spirit of the Lord human weakness (in socio-political sense) is transformed into evangelical *kenosis*. This approach becomes efficacious and fruitful on two preconditions. First, it presupposes that the missionaries believe in the people to whom they are sent. If you have nothing in your hand, and if you do not have any kind of superiority, then you have to rely on the people to whom you are sent. Missionaries are expected to work not simply for the people (from a position of superiority), but to work with the people. Above all, this approach presupposes that missionaries believe in the One who calls and sends them. "I am with you always to the end of time" (Mt 28:20).

Whatever the merit of Kleden's analysis of Asian mission, he usefully highlights one aspect of Christian mission, namely, power, or the lack thereof. If mission is to be divested of its images of political, cultural, economic, and religious dominance, it must be taken up from the perspective of "weakness" in the sense that the missionary must rely on and listen to the people to whom she or he is sent. This significantly shifts the task of mission as educating the natives to being educated by the natives. The missionary has no choice but to be attentive to the context in which he or she is present. This "empty-handed" approach, as Kleden calls it, rejects the use of power in mission to determine beforehand the parameters of the conversation between the evangelizers and the evangelized and views mission as service to the evangelized (and Kleden claims that it must be an active contemplative service).

Kleden here echoes what Leonardo Boff has written in his book *Church, Charism and Power: Liberation Theology and the Institutional Church.*[22] Boff clearly advocates the exercise of church power as service. He cites Mk 10:42–44 and Lk 22:25–27 as examples of how to both understand and exercise power as a Christian: "You know how those who rule the nations exercise tyranny over them and they practice violence against them. This is not to be among you: on the contrary, if one of you wishes to be great, he must be your servant; and he who desires to be first among you must serve all; because the Son of Man did not come to be served but to serve and to give his life for the redemption of many." Boff favors *exousia* (understood as submitting to God's will) over *dynamis* (understood as exercising might) as representing more adequately how power is to be understood and exercised and, by implication, how we should relate with each other. Only in this way can weakness in service become one's strength.

But how is this service in weakness to be understood? Perhaps Jon Sobrino's understanding of the presence and absence of God in the cross of Christ can be of help here. In his *Christology at the Crossroads* Sobrino writes on the death of Jesus and the scandal of the cross. The cross is a scandal because it forces us to raise questions about our concepts of God and who God is in relation to us when God gave us his only Son. For Sobrino, "the path to the cross is nothing else but a questioning search for the true God and for the true essence of power."[23]

Obviously, for Sobrino power is to be used in the service of the oppressed, but what sort of power is at stake? What sort of power makes God present in our midst? The cross of Jesus throws into doubt all the notions we have accrued about the power of God. The event of the cross shows God's power centered in suffering and love. More than this, "we see God submerged in the negative."[24] Indeed, on the cross, God is against himself, God questions God. According to Sobrino, God "bifurcates" himself on the cross so that "transcendence is in conflict with history." To quote Sobrino again: "On the cross of Jesus God was present and at the same time absent. Absent to the son, he was present for human beings. And in this dialectic of presence and absence is the way to express in human language the fact that God is love. The cross is the contradiction of humanity, but it is grounded on an ultimate solidarity with it."[25]

In God's abandonment of Jesus we have the ground for solidarity and relationship at the deepest level between God and humanity. In this solidarity love is born out of and in the midst of suffering. Perhaps we can understand Kleden's empty-handed approach in this light. It is precisely the abandonment of power as *dynamis* (control and might) that allows the true power of solidarity and love to be present. Genuine power in this sense always flows from conditions wherein one has no choice but to act with and on behalf of those one loves. True power is not a choice but a "forced option" that is necessary for genuine relationships and meaningful dialogue. In this context, the Christian *vocatio* begins to take shape in a specific manner. Engaging with persons out of love demands a clear acknowledgment of the contours and shapes of their suffering and pain. Genuine dialogue is only possible when power is exercised as engaging the suffering of loved ones with a view to transforming that void and pain into the presence of God's grace.

OUR CONTEXT AS "FORCED"

This empty-handed approach or service in weakness could be considered as the call and challenge of the Caribbean Church. But what is the context or space in the Caribbean in which this relationship of solidarity and love for others is to take place? This context could be characterized as "forced."[26] It is not necessary to repeat the arguments I made for this concept of "forced context." Here I simply want to show how I arrived at this concept.

My notion of "forced context" was occasioned by the reading of a book on Christ as companion of our life journey by a theologian with Cuban heritage. In it the author cited examples of popular religiosity in Mexico and not in Cuba. This is curious, especially since Christianity and its popular expressions are very much alive in Cuba. This led me to question why the author ignored the obvious religious expressions of Cuba, where his ethnic and cultural roots lie, and used those of Mexico instead. Perhaps his use of Mexico was dictated by political, economic, and social constraints since the Cuban community in the United States by and large opposes Castro's regime. It dawned on me that he was forced (in the sense that he felt constrained) to ignore the Cuban context and had to find an analogous context in Mexico to ground his theological reflections.

It then struck me that in many ways the Caribbean people were and still are "forced" to think in contexts other than their own. That is why people of the Caribbean have to and are able to negotiate multiple relationships at different levels. I attempted to make this forced context theologically relevant by turning traditional philosophical and theological categories on their heads in order to provoke an "alternative consciousness."[27]

The first category I turned on its head is the traditional understanding of free will. I argued that the genuine option for the suffering person is not the result of reasonable choices made by exercising freewill. Furthermore, I argued that will and freedom are not mutually compatible, because meaningful human actions are based not on the possibility and availability of choices but on the lack thereof. For instance, we do theology because it must be done. We have a church because we must witness to God's grace in the midst of our suffering, not merely because a church is a nice thing to have. Our actions are determined not by the possibilities before us but by the urgency of our present condition. Freedom is therefore not dependent on the possibility of new and alternative structures, but on our resistance to present conditions of suffering and exploitation.

The second idea I modified is the notion that freedom and hope are necessary partners. If the condition of being forced propels us to identify what is urgent in our current situation and to realize it, then hope can often deprive us of an understanding of our here and now context. It would be better to fully recognize our forced and desperate situation created by exploitation and suffering than to rely on a hope that might deceive and paralyze us. Hence, we should, paradoxically, understand freedom not in the light of hope but in the context of despair.

The third concept I challenged is the very individualistic way in which we understand what it means to be human and, by extension, faith. Our traditional concept of human nature is based on the presupposition that human nature and identity are grounded in the individual as a singular being. By contrast, I claimed that the forced context calls for a different understanding of the human condition, the basis of which is not the individual but the community. It is only because of the other person(s) that I have a meaningful *human* existence. Hence, to be most fully human and most fully free, one must be in solidarity with others.

It is to be noted that in forced contexts caused by exploitation and suffering people are often tempted to equate religion, religious experience, and theology with the struggle for survival. This identification loses sight of the fact that at times salvation in the Christian understanding denies even the possibility of survival. Indeed, at times, salvation demands death, the closure of all possibility. Our equation of religion with survival, and now, with success, has blinded us to the important difference between survival and salvation. The religion of survival speaks the language of freedom but does not add any specific theological elements to the historical struggle for survival. It remains an Old Testament dispensation.[28] We need a theology of salvation more than we need a theology of survival.

If this is the Caribbean context theologically considered, then what is the Caribbean Church theologically considered? Understanding historical and cultural space in terms of discontinuity, viewing *vocatio* as making present God's grace in the midst of our complex existence, and characterizing that existence as forced, how do we proclaim the church? Looking at our context in its stark reality as forced, recognizing that our survival is only possible in community, and knowing that this survival is only meaningful in terms of salvation, we must conclude that if the Caribbean Church reflects who and what the Caribbean is, it also must take on a forced character. Insofar as it takes on the characteristics of a forced context, it too is determined by the urgency of the Caribbean situation and therefore does not have a choice except to make an option that signals its commitment to and love of the region and its people. This means that the Church in the Caribbean must make a clear option which can be used as the basis for its being and action.

Perhaps I need to state that an option is not the same as a choice. In relating to God and one another one can choose to love or not to love, but though we are free to commit ourselves as we please, we are not free not to love if we claim to be committed to a God of love. In this sense we must make an option to love and are not free to choose otherwise, though it is possible that we could.[29] In a similar manner, by speaking of an option, I want to briefly outline a way for the Caribbean Church to be and act as a genuinely local church.

CHURCH IN THE CARIBBEAN: WHAT OPTION?

In a short essay entitled "The Limbo Gateway,"[30] Wilson Harris explores a philosophy of history for the Caribbean. He sees in the African myth of limbo "a certain kind of gateway or threshold to a new world and the dislocation of a chain of miles."[31] For Harris, *limbo* is a new sensibility that can translate and "accommodate African and other legacies within a new architecture of cultures." He goes on to say: "It is my view—a deeply considered one—that this ground of accommodation, this art of creative coexistence born of great peril and strangest capacity for renewal—pointing away from apartheid and ghetto fixations—is of the utmost importance and *native* to the Caribbean, perhaps to the Americas as a whole."[32] This art of creative coexistence is created by as well as creates a "dislocation of interior space" which serves "as a corrective to a uniform cloak or documentary stasis of imperialism."[33]

What is interesting in Harris's essay is the use of the notion of dislocation and how it takes on positive and negative aspects. In a departure from him, I would like to use the term to describe not just physical and mental space but a people as a whole. I think dislocation historicizes the discontinuity characteristic of the historical, cultural, and cultural context of the Caribbean, and also adequately describes the nature and state of its current context. As a result, the Caribbean Church should be an option for the dislocated.

If the church is to make an option for the dislocated, this option must be supported and clarified by scripture. The first step is to explore how the word of God sheds light on it. In the Old Testament the most obvious text that speaks of a dislocated people is Psalm 137, often called "the Ballad of the Exiles." As the Israelites sit by the rivers of Babylon, they contemplate their fate in exile which makes them cling closer to their God and the land he had given them. Genesis 4:14 presents another understanding of dislocation where God makes Cain a fugitive and a wanderer as a punishment for killing his brother Abel. In antiquity, if you do not belong to a group, you would most likely be a thief or at least a criminal and therefore subject to retribution. Upon Cain's request, God gives him a mark to warn others that God's retribution will be severe if anyone harms Cain. Genesis 12:1 gives yet another context for dislocation: Abraham is called to leave his country and familial relations for a land God will show him. God's order here is interesting. It is difficult for Abraham because he is called to leave not just his country but also his father's house (that is, his immediate family). Thus the order extends not only to land but also to relations. In Exodus 2:22 Moses names his son Gershom because he is a stranger in a foreign land, indicating the difficulty Moses experiences in his exile from Egypt.

In the New Testament it is difficult to pinpoint specific passages that address dislocation. However, it can be said that because he was rejected by his own people, Jesus was forced to preach his message outside of his hometown of Nazareth. Perhaps the parable of the lost (prodigal) son (Lk 15:11–32) is of interest. In this parable, the dislocation made explicit in the younger son's departure and return takes on many different shades when considered in the context of the relationships between the father and the younger son, the father and the older son, and the two brothers. These texts and others need to be studied for the light they can throw on the option for the dislocated.

Second, as part of the research on areas where people have experienced massive dislocation, contemporary post-colonial theory contributes to a better understanding of the situation of dislocation in the Caribbean and in other parts of the world. Further analysis of the post-colonial and globalized context of the world and in particular of the Caribbean is needed. More accurate knowledge of the social, political, economic, and cultural factors at work in the Caribbean is required. In addition, the use of historical analysis developed by those who use the third approach to theology mentioned above will also be helpful to understand dislocation.

Third, dislocation can also be seen as freedom to relocate. Investigation into immigration patterns and trends in and from the region is needed. Contemporary studies on displaced populations and immigrant communities will shed light on a significant aspect of Caribbean reality. A common joke about Trinidadians going home to celebrate the new millennium says that if all Trinidadians were to return home, the island would sink because there seems to be more Trinidadians outside than in Trinidad. The same can be said of any other Caribbean island or territory.

Fourth, dislocation spawns complex relationships and forces persons to inhabit multiple worlds and religions, often at the same time. Some understanding of the nature and range of human relationships among dislocated people is needed. The conference on "Catholic Theology in the Caribbean Today" has been doing some of this work by looking at sexuality (Barbados 2002) and violence (Guyana 2001) and ongoing research projects on religious and interreligious phenomena in the region. Of interest here is how to describe the multiple modes of belonging Caribbean peoples engage and the multiple worlds they inhabit in the region.

Fifth, to root this option for the dislocated in a broad theological context there must be developed a theology of grace that shows how such grace is possible for a dislocated people. In this regard the following statement by Roger Haight is helpful:

> When salvation is conceived of in terms of grace, one focuses on the concrete and historical manifestations of the effects of God's love within the Christian economy. This is certainly the dominant concept of the New Testament itself, for the primitive community of faith was

constituted by the pouring out of the Spirit and lived in the experiential enthusiasm of its gifts and charisms. Here then salvation appears as an economy, a working of God in a history of human events.[34]

To be graced in any context is no mysterious phenomenon. Grace is manifested in our concrete ways of relating and acting. The theology of grace will demystify how God's grace can be made present in dislocation. A Caribbean Church that makes an option for the dislocated makes an option for the Caribbean people as they are.

ECCLESIOLOGICAL IMPLICATIONS

To conclude, I will briefly mention some implications of our foregoing reflections on forced context and dislocation for ecclesiology. First and foremost is the issue of power and its use. Irrespective of space and time, relations of power (and of powerlessness) have defined the nature and role of the church as well as the range and frequency of people's dislocation. I have argued that power in the church must be understood as *exousia*, that is, action done in submission to God's will. Following Kleden, I have called this action an empty-handed approach, which is modeled on Jesus' *kenosis* [self-emptying] (Phil. 2:7). Though traditionally used to refer to the Christ event, *kenosis* is helpful to understand the nature of the church.

Second, dislocation recalls the notion of God's abandonment that Jon Sobrino uses to describe Jesus' death on the cross. Jesus' "abandonment" by God, which is an act of love and solidarity, echoes the empty-handed approach and affirms the necessity of solidarity with others. Christian spirituality is therefore communitarian and not individualistic. The church is not exclusive but inclusive and universal.

Third, insofar as solidarity with others is necessary for what the church must be, the notion of catholicity requires reconsideration. The catholicity or universality of the church implies that community is not simply a collection of individuals but is constituted by the common good of the whole humanity.

Finally, a theology of grace in the context of dislocation offers a new understanding of the holiness of the church. It emphasizes that the church is holy, yet at the same time is sinful. The church as a sacrament—sign and instrument—of salvation exists in the midst of sin. Such is the reality of grace and salvation in forced contexts and amidst dislocated peoples.

NOTES

1. See Gerald Boodoo, "Christologies: Caribbean," in *Dictionary of Third World Theologies*, ed. Virginia Fabella and R. S. Sugirtharajah (Maryknoll, N.Y.: Orbis Books, 2000), 52–53; and Jason Gordon, "Clash of Paradigms: Report from the Caribbean," in *Liberation Theologies on Shifting Grounds: A Clash of Socio-Economic and Cultural Paradigms*, ed. George DeSchrijver (Leuven: Leuven University Press, 1998), 365–79.

2. See *Theology in the Caribbean Today 1*, ed. Patrick Anthony (St. Lucia: Optimum Printers, 1995), 31–38.

3. *Theology in the Caribbean Today 1*, 33.

4. *Theology in the Caribbean Today 1*, 37.

5. See *Theology in the Caribbean Today 1*, 5–30.

6. *Theology in the Caribbean Today 1*, "From Dominance to Partnership: The Christian Community as Locus and Agent of Ministerial Formation," 39–64.

7. *Theology in the Caribbean Today 1*, 53.

8. See *Theology in the Caribbean Today 1*, 65–74.

9. *Theology in the Caribbean Today 1*, 75–81.

10. *Theology in the Caribbean Today 1*, 82–100.

11. *Theology in the Caribbean Today 1*, 97.

12. *Theology in the Caribbean Today 1*, 101–20.

13. *Theology in the Caribbean Today 1*, 112.

14. *Theology in the Caribbean Today 1*, 121–26.

15. *Theology in the Caribbean Today 1*, 126.

16. *Theology in the Caribbean Today 1*, 57.

17. *Theology in the Caribbean Today 1*, 124.

18. Walter Bauer, *A Greek-English Lexicon of the New Testament and Other Early Christian Literature*, second edition, trans. and augmented by William F. Arndt and F. Wilbur Gringrich (Chicago: University of Chicago Press, 1957, 1979), 435–36.

19. Gustavo Gutierrez, *A Theology of Liberation: History, Politics and Salvation*, 15th anniversary edition (Maryknoll, N.Y.: Orbis Books, 1988), 3–12.

20. Gutierrez, *A Theology of Liberation*, 10.

21. *Proceedings of the Fifty-Second Annual Convention of the Catholic Theological Society of America*, vol. 56, ed. Richard Sparks (Milwaukee, Wisc., June 7–10, 2001), 197–98.

22. Leonardo Boff, *Church, Charism and Power: Liberation Theology and the Institutional Church* (London: SCM Press, 1985).

23. Jon Sobrino, *Christology at the Crossroads* (Maryknoll, N.Y.: Orbis Books, 1978), 204.

24. Sobrino, *Christology at the Crossroads,* 221.

25. Sobrino, *Christology at the Crossroads,* 225.

26. I have elaborated on this space in "Gospel and Culture in a Forced Theological Context," *Caribbean Journal of Religious Studies* 17, no. 2 (1996); and

"Paradigm Shift?" in *Liberation Theologies on Shifting Grounds: A Clash of Socio-Economic and Cultural Paradigms*, ed. G. DeSchrijver (Leuven: Leuven University Press, 1998).

27. For the concept of "alternative consciousness," see Joseph Harris's use of Brueggemann in *Theology in the Caribbean Today 1*, 46.

28. Clyde Harvey used this term at our 1998 "Faces of Jesus" conference in Jamaica. He was referring to how political figures used the messianic theme in their rhetoric and presentation of their (and our) understanding of Christianity while holding on to an Old Testament dispensation.

29. See Gustavo Gutiérrez' explanation of this distinction in his *A Theology of Liberation: History, Politics and Salvation*, 15th anniversary edition (Maryknoll, N.Y.: Orbis Books, 1988), xxvi.

30. Wilson Harris, "The Limbo Gateway," in *The Post-Colonial Studies Reader*, ed. Bill Ashcroft, Gareth Griffins, and Helen Tiffin (New York: Routledge, 1995), 378–82.

31. Harris, "The Limbo Gateway," 379.

32. Harris, "The Limbo Gateway," 380.

33. Harris, "The Limbo Gateway," 381.

34. Roger Haight, *The Experience and Language of Grace* (New York: Paulist Press, 1979), 165.

SELECTED BIBLIOGRAPHY

Only a very selective bibliography can be given here. The following items are chosen because they themselves contain further extensive bibliographies that should be consulted.

HISTORY

Burns, Jeffrey M., Ellen Skerrett, and Joseph M. White, eds. *Keeping Faith: European and Asian Catholic Immigrants*. Maryknoll, N.Y.: Orbis Books, 2000.

Dolan, Day P. *In Search of an American Catholicism: A History of Religion and Culture in Tension*. New York: Oxford University Press, 2000.

Gillis, Chester. *Roman Catholicism in America*. New York: Columbia University Press, 1999.

Morris, Charles. *American Catholic: The Saints and Sinners Who Built America's Most Powerful Church*. New York: Vintage Books, 1997.

O'Brien, David J. *Public Catholicism*. Maryknoll, N.Y.: Orbis Books, 1996.

BLACK THEOLOGY

Cone, James H., and Gayraud S. Wilmore, eds. *Black Theology: A Documentary History. Volume One: 1966–1979*. Second edition, revised. Maryknoll, N.Y.: Orbis Books, 1993.

———. *Black Theology: A Documentary History. Volume Two: 1980–1992*. Second edition, revised. Maryknoll, N.Y.: Orbis Books, 1993.

Davis, Cyprian. *The History of Black Catholics in the United States*. New York: Crossroad, 1992.

Hayes, Diana L., and Cyprian Davis, eds. *Taking Down Our Harp: Black Catholics in the United States.* Maryknoll, N.Y.: Orbis Books, 1998. *Theological Studies* 61, no. 4 (2000).

LATINO/HISPANIC THEOLOGY

De La Torre, Miguel A., and Edwin David Aponte. *Introducing Latino/A Theologies.* Maryknoll, N.Y.: Orbis Books, 2001.
Espín, Orlando O., and Miguel H. Díaz, eds. *From the Heart of Our People: Latino/a Explorations Catholic Systematic Theology.* Maryknoll, N.Y.: Orbis Books, 1999.

ASIAN AMERICAN THEOLOGY

Park, Andrew Sung. *Racial Conflict & Healing: An Asian-American Theological Perspective.* Maryknoll, N.Y.: Orbis Books, 1996.
Phan, Peter C. *Christianity with an Asian Face: Asian American Theology in the Making.* Maryknoll, N.Y.: Orbis Books, 2003.
Phan, Peter C., and Yung Young Lee, eds. *Journeys at the Margin: Toward an Autobiographical Theology in American-Asian Perspective.* Collegeville, Minn.: The Liturgical Press, 1999.

CARIBBEAN THEOLOGY

Anthony, Patrick, ed. *Theology in the Caribbean Today 1: Perspectives.* St. Lucia: Archdiocesan Pastoral Centre, 1994.
Erskine, Noel Leo. *Decolonizing Theology: A Caribbean Perspective.* Maryknoll, N.Y.: Orbis Books, 1981.
Gregory, Howard, ed. *Caribbean Theology: Preparing for the Challenges Ahead.* Jamaica: Canoe Press, University of the West Indies, 1995.

NATIVE AMERICAN THEOLOGY

Kidwell, Clara Sue, Homer Noley, and George E. "Tink" Tinker, eds. *A Native American Theology.* Maryknoll, N.Y.: Orbis Books, 2001.
Weaver, Jace, ed. *Native American Religious Identity: Unforgotten Gods.* Maryknoll, N.Y.: Orbis Books, 1998.

INDEX

ABOUT THE CONTRIBUTORS

Gerald Boodoo, Ph.D., is professor of theology at Xavier University of Louisiana.

Kevin Burke, S.J., S.T.D., is associate professor of systematic theology at Weston Jesuit School of Theology, Cambridge, Massachusetts. He is the author of *The Ground Beneath the Cross: The Theology of Ignacio Ellacuría* (2000).

Roberto Goizueta, Ph.D., is professor of theology at Boston College. He is the author of *Caminemos con Jesús: Toward a Hispanic/Latino Theology of Accompaniment* (1995).

Diana Hayes, J.D., Ph.D., S.T.D., is associate professor of theology at Georgetown University. She is the author of many books including *Hagar's Daughters: Womanist Ways of Being in the World* (1995) and *And Still We Rise: An Introduction to Black Liberation Theology* (1996).

Peter C. Phan, S.T.D., Ph.D., D.D., is the Ignacio Ellacuría Professor of Catholic Social Thought at Georgetown University. He is the author of many books including the trilogy: *Christianity with an Asian Face* (2003); *In Our Tongues* (2003); and *Being Religious Interreligiously* (2004).

Jeanette Rodriguez, Ph.D., is professor of theological studies at Seattle University. Among her many publications is *Our Lady of Guadalupe: Faith and Empowerment among Mexican-American Women* (1994).

Mark Stelzer, S.T.D., is acting president and adjunct professor of theology at Elms College.